This is the light of the mind

SELECTIONS FROM THE Sylvia Plath

COLLECTION OF Judith G. Raymo

NEW YORK The Grolier Club

2017

Catalogue of an exhibition held at the Grolier Club,
September 19 – November 4, 2017.

"This is the light of the mind" is from the first line of "The Moon and the Yew Tree," published in *Ariel* (1965), a volume of poems by Sylvia Plath (cat. 8).

ISBN 978-1-60583-071-1

PHOTO CREDITS:
Cover and page 16 courtesy of College Archives, Smith College,
Northampton, MA.
Pages 40 and 70 by Helen Glazer.
All other photography by Robert Lorenzson, New York.

COVER: Sylvia Plath (1955).

Contents

ACKNOWLEDGMENTS

In the course of developing this exhibition, I have visited four archives that hold the manuscripts, letters, journals, books, ephemera and other materials of, and relating to, both Sylvia Plath and Ted Hughes. I extend my appreciation and thanks to Karen Kukil, who has given so generously of her time and expertise during my many visits to the Mortimer Rare Book Room at Smith College and who has kindly enabled me to display some of those materials in this exhibition. Karen's curatorial assistant, Katie Mikulka, has shared her knowledge of Plath's works, answering my queries accurately and with good humor. I also thank Martin Antonetti, Barbara Blumenthal, Beth Meyers, and Nancy Young for facilitating my research during my visits to the Smith archives. Special thanks to Peter Steinberg for his encyclopedic knowledge of everything Plath, his thoughtful responses to my e-mails, and his patient proofing of this text. I am also grateful to Heather Clark, now completing a literary biography of Plath, who has generously shared her expertise with me and from whom I have learned so much during this past year. Thanks are also due to Cherry Williams and her staff at the Lilly Library in Bloomington, Indiana for the courtesies extended to me while researching its rich collection of Plath materials, and Kathy Shoemaker and her staff at the Rose Manuscript, Archives and Rare Book Library at Emory University in Atlanta for welcoming me to its extensive collection of the papers of Ted Hughes. I spent a productive day in the manuscript room of the British Library, researching additional materials in its holdings of the papers of various associates of Plath and Hughes. Amanda Ferrara has provided support and assistance to me, first as a Smith undergraduate when we worked together in presenting the Grolier Club Poetry Evening on Sylvia Plath in 2012, and during this past year, as an archivist in the Nielsen Library at Smith, working with me in designing this exhibition. Javier Milligan has also provided valuable technical expertise that has facilitated this process. Many thanks to Lisa Baskin, who provided insights borne of the friendship that she and her late husband, Leonard, shared with the Hughes family, and who has generously enabled me to include reproductions of some of Leonard Baskin's illustrations in this catalogue. The Grolier Club has facilitated this exhibition in many ways: Jennifer Sheehan, the exhibitions director has offered patient oversight of every aspect; Eric Holzenberg, the club's executive director has given expert advice on its planning and execution; and Fern Cohen and the members of Members' Exhibition Committee have provided their expertise for its installation—to each of them, my sincere thanks. Finally, I thank Richard Larschan and Rose Goldemberg, who shared with me their recollections of Aurelia Plath; Amanda Golden, David Trinidad, and Elizabeth Winder, three Plath scholars whose advice and counsel have been invaluable; and Jonathan Rabinowitz, Carolyn and Ward Smith, and my friends at Poets House who have enhanced my awareness and understanding of poets and poetry—truly a transformative experience.

Introduction

I have been collecting editions of the work of the poet Sylvia Plath for twenty-five years. My early interest was sparked by the posthumous publication of her extraordinary book of poems, *Ariel* (1965). Plath and I were both undergraduates who majored in English literature at Smith College in the 1950s, and as I began to collect her works in earnest and to read the many accounts of her life, I reflected on the experiences of young women who came of age in post-World War II society as we sought to negotiate the often-conflicting expectations and challenges of mid-twentieth-century culture. We know the many details of Plath's daily existence from her remarkably candid journals, in which she recorded her thoughts, experiences, and drafts of poetry and fiction from the age of eleven. When read in tandem with her correspondence to her mother, her friends and her family, these documents provide us with an abundant record of a writer's interior and private life and its many turning points.

Sylvia Plath was the daughter of an entomologist—Otto Plath—who had immigrated to the US from East Prussia as a teenager, and whose special interest was bees and beekeeping. He was twice the age of Sylvia's mother, Aurelia Plath; they met when she took a graduate course with him at Boston University. Sylvia had a younger brother, Warren, and the family unit lived near her maternal grandparents in the seaside town of Winthrop, Massachusetts. Her father's death from untreated diabetes nine days after her eighth birthday was a traumatic event for Sylvia, perceived by literary critics as influencing the nature and direction of much of her poetry. In a brief memoir of this phase of her life, she recalled: "My father died; we moved inland. Whereon those first nine years of my life sealed themselves off like a ship in a bottle—beautiful, inaccessible, obsolete, a fine white flying myth."[1] Both the memory of his death and the myth she created about him were continuously reconstituted throughout her life. Helen Vendler, the literary critic, identified nineteen early poems and four later elegies written by Plath about her father.[2] Following his death, the family moved to a smaller home in Wellesley, Massachusetts, where Sylvia and her mother shared a bedroom until her sixteenth year, when her brother left for boarding school. Family resources had been depleted in caring for her father, and Aurelia Plath entered the workforce as a teacher, and later college instructor, at Boston University's School of Practical Arts; despite bouts of poor health, she remained at BU until her retirement.

Plath and her mother had a complex relationship, and Aurelia became her daughter's confidant, advisor, and unequivocal supporter. They exchanged over a thousand letters throughout Sylvia's life; I've included one example in this exhibition, a greeting card that opens to display a typed letter (cat. 17). Sylvia viewed herself as an artist as well as a poet, and in her freshman year at Smith College, contemplated a major in studio art. She began to write while quite young, publishing her first poem in the *Boston Herald* in 1941. Encouraged by her mother and her teachers, she submitted poems and stories throughout her pre-college and college years, keeping a meticulous record of drafts circulated to specific periodicals and contests, and the acceptances, rejections, and prizes awarded. This process accelerated when she enrolled at Smith on a scholarship partially funded by Olive Higgins Prouty, the author of romance novels that included *Now, Voyager* and *Stella Dallas,* who became a lifelong friend and benefactor.

Smith's culture in the fifties was a curious combination of honor codes and strict *in loco parentis* rules exemplified by housemothers, un-proctored examinations, nightly curfews, limited off-campus travel on weekends, and compulsory attendance at weekly chapel chaired by the college's president. Smith was known informally as one of the Seven Sisters, an appellation given to colleges in the northeastern United States that had been founded to provide women with academically rigorous liberal arts programs of a quality comparable to the men's colleges of the Ivy League. Women's values in mid-twentieth-century America were characterized by one of Plath's contemporaries—the poet Adrienne Rich—as "the family-centered, consumer-oriented, Freudian American world of the 1950s."[3] To be professionally ambitious meant challenging the entrenched establishment that viewed young women as submissive, refined, and fulfilling appropriate pursuits.

Plath's writing talent and work ethic were noted early in her college years. In her junior year, she was named editor of the college's literary magazine—*Smith Review*—also winning the *Mademoiselle* magazine fiction prize of $500 for her story, "Sunday at the Mintons'" (cat. 16). A voracious reader, her journals and letters home reflect her seriousness of purpose and her goal of gaining acceptance at prestigious magazines such as *Harper's, The Atlantic,* and above all, *The New Yorker.* At the same time, she expressed the desire to earn a living by writing for popular women's magazines. She read widely among women poets, including Emily Dickinson, Amy Lowell, Marianne Moore, Edith Sitwell and others, as well as women novelists in the literary canon: Jane Austen, Charlotte and Emily Bronte, George Eliot, and Virginia Woolf. A major setback occurred in late August 1953 when Plath attempted suicide by swallowing an overdose of her mother's sleeping pills. Her ironic and biting account of this event and its aftermath, highlighted by her four-month hospitalization at McLean Hospital, are contained in her autobiographical novel, *The Bell Jar* (first published under a pseudonym in 1963). She returned to Smith in February 1954, ultimately graduating Phi Beta Kappa and *summa cum laude* in June 1955. With support from two of her English professors, Mary Ellen Chase and Elizabeth Drew, she was awarded a Fulbright scholarship to read English for two years at Newnham College, Cambridge.

This phase of Plath's development proved decisive, since it was at Cambridge that, midway through her matriculation, she met and married a budding poet from Yorkshire named Edward James (Ted) Hughes. He had recently completed his studies in anthropology and was contemplating relocation to Australia where his older brother, Gerald, had settled. In her journal, Sylvia describes the "big, dark, hunky boy, the only one there huge enough for me" (UJ, 211), and their meeting at a launch party for a new poetry magazine—*Saint Botolph's Review* (cat. 13)—in which he had published three poems that caught her attention. In a letter to his sister, Olwyn, Hughes declared "I have met a first-rate American poetess ... one of the best female poets I ever read."[4] We know about this meeting and much about the events that followed from her vivid journal entries. Within four months of their first meeting, Sylvia and Ted Hughes married, on June 16, 1956 (Bloomsday in James Joyce's *Ulysses*) in the Church of St. George the Martyr in Bloomsbury. Aurelia Plath, who had come to England for a visit, was the sole witness. Hughes writes of that day in the poem, "A Pink Wool Knitted Dress," one of eighty-eight poems contained in *Birthday Letters,* his only personal account of their marriage. Written over a period of twenty-five years, it was published in 1998, nine months prior to his death from colon cancer.

Following completion of her second year at Cambridge and having obtained a teaching position at her alma mater, Smith College, the couple sailed for New York on the *Queen Elizabeth* in June 1957. After spending the summer on Cape Cod, a wedding gift from her mother, Sylvia Plath took up her new position at Smith as an instructor in English literature. Through journal entries, we know that she found daunting the combined pressures of teaching, writing, and married life. Hughes, who taught part-time at the University of Massachusetts in Amherst, viewed writing as a full-time occupation, and thus, at the conclusion of a year of teaching in her bid for independence and a creative partnership with Hughes, Sylvia rejected a continuing appointment in Smith's English department.

There followed a year among Boston's writing community, travel throughout the western United States with brief stops in Canada and Mexico, and eleven-week fellowships for Ted and Sylvia at Yaddo, the writing colony in Saratoga Springs, New York.

The couple returned to London five months prior to the birth of their daughter, Frieda, and after brief stays with friends and family in Yorkshire and London, they moved into a small flat at 3 Chalcot Square on February 1, 1960. Within a few months, Hughes proposed that they leave the hectic pace of London for a more peaceful family life in the English countryside. After much deliberation about the expenditure of funds for a home outside London, in 1961, with gifts and loans from their mothers, they purchased Court Green, a thatched cottage in Devonshire. Five months later, their son Nicholas was born. Events seemed to spiral out of control in July 1962, when Hughes began an affair with Assia Weevil, whose husband David was also a poet and who had subleased their London flat. This affair led to the Hughes's marital separation in October; it also resulted in a period of manic activity for Sylvia, whose poems took on an urgency and passion borne of her changed status and identity as an American woman, living independently in the English countryside, caring for two young children, and having few material or psychic resources.

In December 1962, Plath moved back to London with her two children into a house at 23 Fitzroy Road that had been occupied at one time by the poet William Butler Yeats. Three months later, on February 11, 1963, while her children slept upstairs, she committed suicide by laying her head inside a gas oven. One month before her death, adopting the pseudonym, Victoria Lucas, she published her novel *The Bell Jar* (cat. 49). At her death, Plath had published hundreds of poems and many short stories in literary journals, magazines, and anthologies, one book of poetry and one novel. However, she became linked in perpetuity to her estranged husband, Ted

Hughes. For it was Hughes who oversaw (with his sister, Olwyn), the selection, editing, and publication of her oeuvre. The circumstances of their marriage and the seven years of their life together have become the stuff of myth and her life and writings have taken on a legendary quality.

Plath's poems and stories have been translated into more than thirty languages. The Modern Language Association database for 2016 contains 1,048 entries for Sylvia Plath: 690 journal articles, 200 book chapters, 70 books, and 88 dissertations.[5] Fictionalized versions of Plath's life have been made into films, plays, novels, and an Italian opera. *The Bell Jar* regularly appears on high school reading lists and *Ariel* is now required reading in many gender studies courses. In 2010, Plath was inducted into Poet's Corner in the Cathedral of St. John the Divine. And in April 2012, she was one of ten American poets honored with his or her image on a US postage stamp. There is also a comprehensive website and blog maintained by Peter K. Steinberg[6] and three new biographies have been published since 2013, all evidence that Sylvia Plath remains an iconic figure whose presence continues to be felt and to inspire younger generations of poets, writers, and artists. *The Letters of Sylvia Plath, Volume I*, edited by Peter K. Steinberg and Karen V. Kukil, will be published by Faber and Faber in England and by HarperCollins in the US in October 2017. *The Letters, Volume II* is scheduled to follow in 2018. In April 2017, the recent discovery of a trove of letters sent by Plath to her psychiatrist was widely reported in the media. These letters are currently the subject of litigation as to their rightful owner and the veracity of their alleged content has not been publicly verified.

In this exhibition, I have selected seventy-eight works and related materials that trace Plath's literary development as a poet and writer. I have sought to focus attention on some of the early influences on her growth as a poet, including annotated editions of books that she read, manuscript drafts and letters, and periodicals in which her work appeared. I have also included items from my collection that demonstrate, in a variety of media, the extent of artistic expression that she has inspired among composers, paint-ers, playwrights, book designers, graphic artists, and poets. Also exhibited are a small selection of photographs and other materi-als that offer visitors both visual and auditory representations of Sylvia Plath.

Sylvia Plath, Marblehead, MA, 24 July 1951.
Courtesy of College Archives, Smith College, Northampton, MA.

Recovering Sylvia Plath

HEATHER CLARK

Since her death in 1963, Sylvia Plath has become a paradoxical symbol of female power and helplessness whose life has been subsumed by her afterlife. Caught in the limbo between icon and cliché, she has been mythologized in movies, television, and biographies as a high priestess of poetry, obsessed with death. These distortions gained momentum in the 1960s when her seminal collection *Ariel* was published just as the details of her suicide became known. Most reviewers didn't know what to make of the burning, pulsating metaphors in poems like "Lady Lazarus," or the chilly imagery of "Edge." *Time* called the book a "jet of flame from a literary dragon."[7] The *Washington Post* dubbed Plath a "snake lady of misery" in an article titled "The Cult of Plath."[8]

Robert Lowell, in his introduction to *Ariel*, characterized Plath as hurtling toward her own destruction. Even Plath's closest reader, her husband Ted Hughes, often portrayed her as a passive vessel through which a dangerous muse spoke. Melodramatic portraits of Plath as a crazed poetic priestess do not seem to be going away anytime soon. Her most recent biographer called her "a sorceress who had the power to attract men with a flash of her intense eyes, a tortured soul whose only destiny was death by her own hand."[9] He wrote that she "aspired to transform herself into a psychotic deity."[10]

Sylvia Plath would not have recognized herself in these distorted portraits. She hated depression, and wanted to be strong, passionate, and brave, like a character in a D. H. Lawrence novel. Sometimes she called herself lazy, and exhorted herself to work harder—not because she was a perfectionist, but because she wanted to fulfill the literary potential that depression threatened to annul. She distrusted male psychiatrists, and tried to understand her own depression intellectually, through great works by Fyodor Dostoyevsky, Sigmund Freud, Virginia Woolf, and Thomas Mann. Bitter experience taught her how to accommodate depression—exploit it, even—for the sake of her art. Depression gave her insight into the lives of the outcast, and would lead her to question the link between insanity and cultural repression in her great protest novel, *The Bell Jar*. She would fill her work, sometimes controversially, with the disenfranchised—women, the mentally ill, refugees, political dissidents, Jews, prisoners, divorcées. As she matured she grew more determined to speak out on their behalf, and her own. But she never romanticized depression and death. It was the resurfacing, the rebirth, that interested her.

The Oxford professor Hermione Lee, Virginia Woolf's biographer, has written, "Women writers whose lives involved abuse, mental-illness, self-harm, suicide, have often been treated, biographically, as victims or psychological case-histories first and as professional writers second."[11] This is especially true of Sylvia Plath, who was amongst the most highly educated women of her generation. Even after a suicide attempt and several months of treatment at McLean Hospital, she still managed to graduate from Smith College *summa cum laude*. She was an academic superstar and perennial prizewinner, accepted to graduate programs at Columbia, Oxford, and Radcliffe. She won a Fulbright Fellowship to Newnham College, Cambridge, where she completed a three-year degree in two years, with high honors. Smith's English department offered her a job, even without a PhD—such was her brilliance. Her mastery of English literature intimidated her students, and even her fellow poets. In Robert Lowell's 1959 writing seminar, her peers remembered how easily she picked up on obscure literary allusions. "'Reminds me of Empson,' she used to say. . . . 'It reminds me of Herbert. Perhaps the early Marianne Moore?'"[12] Later, Plath made small talk with T. S. Eliot and Stephen Spender at London cocktail parties, where she was the model of wit and decorum. Very few friends realized she struggled with depression. She struck most as brilliant, ebullient, a shining golden girl. That Plath is now strongly identified with female hysteria—the very cliché she sought to unravel—is part of her tragedy.

"What happens to a dream deferred?," Langston Hughes asks in his poem "Harlem." Did it "crust and sugar over— / like a syrupy sweet?" For most women of Plath's generation, it did. But Plath was determined to follow her literary vocation. She dreaded the condescending label of "lady poet," and had no intention of remaining single and childless like Marianne Moore and Elizabeth Bishop. She wanted to be a wife, mother, and poet—spheres that hardly ever overlapped in the 1950s. For a time, it seemed she might successfully integrate all three roles. Then, in the autumn of 1962, Ted Hughes left her for another woman. The edifice fell, but the poetry came fast and strong. Alone with her two young children in rural England, she began writing the poems that would, as she predicted, make her name.

Her early, formally intricate poems like "Go Get the Goodly Squab" (cat. 11), helped her achieve modest success. The new *Ariel* poems, with their speed, daring, and bravado, and their rage against personal and historical oppressions, sounded a new note in postwar poetry. Poems like "Lady Lazarus," "The Applicant," and "Daddy" seethe at the sexist prescriptions of Plath's society, while "Edge" takes the ideal of feminine passivity to its extreme, conceding with a cool, horrific irony that only a dead woman is "perfected." Plath died eight days before Betty Friedan's *The Feminine Mystique* was published, but her work broke through a literary glass ceiling. It was as if she had scored the emerging women's liberation movement to poetry.

Over fifty years after her death, Plath's poems now seem locked in a fixed context: "confessional," "feminist." Yet she wrote her poems before these terms existed. Plath's persona has been too closely aligned with *The Bell Jar*, a staple of high school reading lists, and a small number of poems that feminism—and the feminist backlash—made famous. The vengeful heroines of "Daddy," "Purdah," and "Lady Lazarus," and the Medea figure of "Edge," are not Sylvia Plath but fictional creations. A new generation of literary critics has begun to reveal a more nuanced version of Plath. Blinded by the details of her suicide and the seemingly "confessional" nature of her poems, we are now more aware of how Plath's life and work have become ciphers for cultural anxieties about women and power. We now see that she was a master of disguise and irony who used the confessional mode to expose her readers' lust for sensational details from her life—as in "Lady Lazarus," where the heroine performs a strip-tease for the "peanut crunching crowd" come to watch another suicide. "Lady Lazarus," which practically predicts reality television, is cultural commentary masking as autobiography. Plath understood, ahead of her time, the allure of the tabloid, which she mocked and exploited in her own writing. We see more clearly, too, how the influence of Cold War politics, environmental concerns, modern art—especially the surrealism of Paul Klee and Giorgio de Chirico—shaped her work. Plath's short story, "Mary Ventura and the Ninth Kingdom" (cat. 51), shows her experimenting with surrealism early in her career.

The "confessional" label also simplifies Plath's deep engagement with the English literary tradition, which she mastered at Smith and Cambridge. Plath read female writers like Virginia Woolf, Marianne Moore, Elizabeth Bishop, Sarah Teasdale, Edna St. Vincent Millay, Edith Sitwell, and Anne Sexton, but her academic education was grounded in male modernism. The psychological and anthropological writings of Carl Jung, Robert Graves, and James Frazer, as well as the poetry and prose of W. B. Yeats, Dylan Thomas, Wallace

Stevens, James Joyce, T. S. Eliot, W. H. Auden, and Robert Lowell, were the bedrock upon which she built her scaffolding. Jane Baltzell Kopp, an American who befriended Sylvia Plath and Ted Hughes at Cambridge in 1955–56, spoke of the importance of "the old, High Culture" education they all experienced together. "We were then as unconscious of the fact as fish are of water, but *that tradition had everything to do with the way we in those days all saw ourselves, each other, and our lives.* . . . At almost every moment, in other words, we were seeing ourselves *sub specie aeternitatis.*"[13] Anyone interested in understanding Sylvia Plath's poetry, Kopp pointed out, would learn more by studying her English Tripos exam at Cambridge than by probing her relationship with her dead father. "The amount—and range—of reading implied by those questions tells the tale."[14]

Ironically, Plath's "confessional" poems of family trauma, marital problems, and sexual jealousy often engage in a dialogue with this "impersonal" literary tradition that had shut women out. The allusions to T. S. Eliot's "The Waste Land" in "Daddy" are easy to miss amidst the poem's many controversies. Likewise, "Edge" responds to Yeats's "He Wishes His Beloved Were Dead," as well as Shakespeare and Robert Graves. *The Bell Jar* uses for its template Joyce's *Portrait of the Artist as a Young Man*, while "Ariel" argues with Ted Hughes's "The Thought-Fox" about the sources of creative inspiration. Plath challenged the male Romantic notion that the moorland outside her door was more sublime than her baby's nursery, and in so doing changed the course of the nature poem. She pioneered the poetry of maternity, opening a new, untapped vein. She is one of the first poets in English to write about miscarriage, abortion, and postpartum anxiety. She redefined the elegy in "The Colossus" and "Daddy," making space for female anger as well as love and pathos. Her poems about depression's ravages—"Tulips," "Elm," "The Moon and the Yew Tree," "Sheep in Fog," "Edge"—are some of the most powerful in the language.

Elizabeth Hardwick once wrote of Plath, "when the curtain goes down, it is her own dead body there on the stage, sacrificed to her own plot."[15] Yet to suggest that Plath's suicide was some sort of grand finale only perpetuates "the Plath myth" that simplifies our understanding of her work and her life. Of course, what makes Sylvia Plath's life compelling to so many readers is its archetypal tragedy. Her life, her fame, and her art will always be tied to her suicide—there is no changing that. But her battles with depression, her heartbreak over her ruptured marriage, and her struggle to raise two toddlers on her own while writing *Ariel* show us that the most famous woman poet of the twentieth century was neither fragile ingénue nor femme fatale. She was no Medea, no Eurydice, no Electra. Rather, she was a highly disciplined craftswoman whose singular voice helped transform American and British literature, and whose innovative work gave new energy to the burgeoning literary and cultural revolutions of her time.

Heather Clark is a Fellow at the Leon Levy Center for Biography at the Graduate Center, CUNY, and a Visiting Fellow at the British Library, the Oxford Centre for Life-Writing, and the University of Huddersfield (UK). She is the author of the award-winning *The Ulster Renaissance: Poetry in Belfast 1962–1972* and *The Grief of Influence: Sylvia Plath and Ted Hughes*, both published by Oxford University Press. She writes regularly for the *Harvard Review*. Her biography of Sylvia Plath will be published by Knopf in 2019.

Catalogue

SELECTIONS FROM CAT. 67–70.

I. Early and Transitional Poems

The placement of Sylvia Plath's poems into early, transitional, and mature categories is somewhat arbitrary, particularly since this process occurred with little evidence of how she would characterize them. Plath published poems and stories in American and British periodicals and anthologies during her life. However, *The Colossus and Other Poems* (cat. 1) was the sole book of poems she saw to fruition before she died. Published in England shortly after she and Ted Hughes returned from the United States, she considered it a major breakthrough in her quest for recognition as a poet. Critic Helen Vendler agrees, asserting that Plath came of age as a poet with *The Colossus,* "casting off the spell of her predecessors—from Dickinson to Dylan Thomas, from Yeats to Lowell ... achieving a style of her own, visible in her condensed symbolic complexes, some as short as a single phrase. She learned to construct a poem by means of grammar, syntax, stanza, shape, and rhythm.... Above all, she learned to mingle wit and tragedy, to permit the contrary emotions of anger and love to fuse in a single lyric."[16]

1. *The Colossus and Other Poems.* London: Heinemann, 1960. First edition.

    The Colossus is Sylvia Plath's first book, published on October 31, 1960. While many of the poems display the neat formalist symmetry typical of her university apprenticeship years, others such as "The Colossus," "Lorelei," "Full Fathom Five," and "The Stones" look forward to the looser cadences of *Ariel* (cat. 8). These poems show Plath assimilating the freer aesthetic of Robert Lowell's *Life Studies* (cat. 56), parts of which she had read in his Boston University seminar in 1959. They also reflect the influence of Anne Sexton and Ted Hughes. *The Colossus* received positive reviews from important London critics. A. Alvarez wrote in *The Observer* of the poems' "ominous, odd" pressure: "It is this sense of threat, as though she were continually menaced by something she could see only out of the corner of her eye, that gives her work its distinction."[17] Yet Plath was disappointed *The Colossus* won no prizes. She wrote to her mother and her brother, Warren, that she worried it would be merely a "nice gift book" for friends and relatives (LH, 400).

2. *The Colossus and Other Poems*. New York: Knopf, 1962.

The American edition of Plath's manuscript was ultimately published by Knopf after the concluding section, "Poem for a Birthday," was shortened and some other changes were made in the sequence of the poems. In a letter to the poetry editor at Knopf, Plath agreed, on the condition that two of the seven sections in the "Birthday" poem be retained: "Flute Notes from a Reedy Pond" and "The Stones," which she felt were integral to the book. "Love is the uniform of my bald nurse' etc., seems to me the way I would like to end the book."[18]

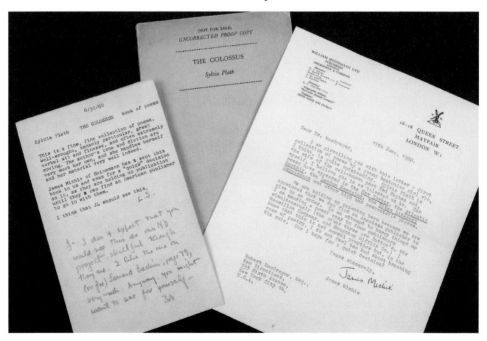

3. *The Colossus and Other Poems.* Uncorrected proof containing 44 poems. With correspondence and notes.

    Among the manuscript material is a letter from James Michie, editor at William Heinemann Ltd., London, dated June 17, 1960 to Robert MacGregor at New Directions publishers: "I am sending a proof copy to four publishers simultaneously" seeking "American publisher to give us an order."[19] Also with internal correspondence by MacGregor commenting favorably on the manuscript ("fine, fine collection of poems"), and noting the request for "quick decision on it (6/30/60)"; plus a second note to MacGregor: "Bob, Sorry this got sidetracked. Not for us, I'd say," [signed] "J." (8/12/60).

4. *Crossing the Water: Transitional Poems.* London: Faber and Faber, 1971.

5. *Winter Trees.* London: Faber and Faber, 1971. First edition.

    Ted Hughes assumed the role of posthumous producer/editor of Plath's legacy with the publication of *Ariel* in 1965. Publication of the English editions of *Crossing the Water* and *Winter Trees* enhanced that legacy. In his introduction to *Winter Trees,* Hughes sought to differentiate the poems he selected from the transitional poems of *Crossing the Water,* asserting that their dark tone and intense imagery foreshadowed the powerful poetic voice of the *Ariel* poems composed in her last months. Hughes added Plath's only verse play, *Three Women,* as the concluding entry in the American edition of *Winter Trees* (1972), stating that it constituted a transition between two poetic voices that defined and differentiated Plath's early and late work. *Crossing the Water* is framed as a collection of Plath's "transitional poems." Hughes included in it nine poems that had been omitted from the American edition of *The Colossus.* For each collection that Hughes edited, he reviewed an assortment of source material—poems that had remained unpublished at Plath's death as well as poems that she had sold to an impressive range of British and American publications, including *The New Yorker, Poetry, Hudson Review, Tri-Quarterly, Harper's, The New Statesmen, London Magazine, The Listener, New American Review, Partisan Review,* and *The Texas Quarterly.* In giving permission to Faber and Faber to publish *Crossing the Water* and *Winter Trees,* Hughes took note of the growing interest in Plath's work among literary scholars, particularly after publication of *Ariel* (1965). It had been Plath's practice to submit each of her poems and stories to British and American periodicals; Hughes took this process to the next level, enabling the publication of collections of selected poems by prestigious publishers and in fine-press editions. More than twenty editions, including fine press and small-press publications were issued between her death and the release of Hughes's edition of *Collected Poems* in 1981. As Stephen Tabor, editor of a comprehensive bibliography of her work, observed, these texts constituted "Plath's posthumous literary career," acquainting scholars and critics with the diversity and power of her poetic expression and further enhancing her literary reputation.[20]

6. *Uncollected Poems.* Turret Booklet No. 2. London: Turret Books, 1965. Printed by Villiers Publications Ltd.

Ten poems representing an intermediate stage in Plath's development, forming a link between *The Colossus* and *Ariel.* It includes Plath's poem "Insomniac," awarded the Cheltenham Festival Guinness Poetry Prize in 1961, a noteworthy event for Plath, since Hughes had also won this prize. One poem, "Half-Moon" (the title was later changed to "Thalidomide") is shown in the centerfold facsimile on pink paper. Hughes selected Plath's 1956 drawing of the West Yorkshire house that had inspired the novel *Wuthering Heights* to decorate the green cover of this booklet. The drawing can be seen as a complement to Plath's poem, "Wuthering Heights," written in 1961.

7. *Three Women: A Poem for Three Voices.* London: Turret Books, 1968. First edition. Privately printed at Oficyna Stanislawa Gilwy, Southend-on-Sea, Essex. No. 70 of 180 copies. Cream-colored cloth, gilt-stamped illustration of three women's heads by Stanislaw Gliwa.

Three aspects make this radio play of special interest. *Three Women* is Plath's only verse play, written specifically for broadcasting. It was produced by Douglas Cleverdon for the BBC Third Programme and broadcast on August 19, 1962. It is seen as having a connection to the imagery of Robert Graves's *The White Goddess* (1948), which Plath and Hughes shared as their common muse, a symbol of their poetic inspiration. Plath wrote to her mother that she was "inspired" to use a maternity ward as the setting, recalling an Ingmar Bergman film, *Brink of Life* (1958) that she had seen in London, "in 1961 or 1962, where it was probably called *So Close to Life*."[21] In this play, written in 1962, three women in an unnamed maternity ward, dressed in hospital gowns and identified only as "First Voice (Wife)," "Second Voice (Secretary)," and "Third Voice (Student)," muse on their personal experiences of pregnancy, childbirth, and miscarriage. Perhaps Plath is evoking her own emotions following the birth of her daughter Frieda in 1960, her miscarriage in 1961, and the birth of her son Nicholas in 1962. Or possibly, this has a more feminist purpose, critiquing the marginalization of women's voices. Third Voice is a student who expresses her ambivalence about giving up her baby for adoption. Unlike Bergman's film, these voices never address each other directly; they alternate in telling their stories to an unseen audience. In her journals, Plath wrote at length about her own feelings as an expectant mother, describing in detail the birth of her son in their Devon home, and the midwife, Winifred Davies, who cared for her (UJ, 645–7). The feminists who founded *Ms.* chose this play for its preview issue in the spring of 1972 (cat. 33).

II. The Plath-Hughes Working Relationship

The working relationship between Sylvia Plath and Ted Hughes throughout their marriage has been well documented by both poets in their letters and journals as well as in their poems and essays. Early in their marriage, Plath explained to her mother that "it is heaven to have someone like Ted who is so kind and honest and brilliant, always stimulating me to study, think, draw, and write" (LH, 289). In this section, I have selected publications that exemplify (either directly or indirectly) their creative partnership, the extent of their influence on each other's work, and for Hughes, the benefits of hindsight that he enjoyed in commenting on and editing Plath's poetry and prose.

8. *Ariel: Poems by Sylvia Plath.* London: Faber and Faber, 1965. First edition.

There are two editions of *Ariel*—Plath's and Hughes's. When Hughes went to Plath's flat following her suicide, he found a neatly stacked manuscript in a black spring binder. It contained forty poems that began with "Morning Song" and ended with "Wintering"—the first word was "love" and the last was "spring." Hughes didn't publish the poems in the order they were found, and replaced twelve poems in the American edition, and thirteen in the English edition, concluding on a note of foreboding and despair with the poems "Edge" and "Words." He selected the replacements from nineteen poems written in the last three months of her life and three earlier poems.[22] Indicative of the frenetic pace of her creative powers, Plath wrote twenty-five major poems in October 1962. Her legacy became the poems written in the Ariel voice, establishing her posthumous reputation as a major poet and a feminist icon. In *Ariel*, the dramatic imagery, relentless in its candor, breaks through constraints that had earlier impeded her work and in the process rewrites the narrative of her adult life. Robert Lowell, whose poetry seminar she attended in the spring of 1959 while in Boston, was asked by Hughes to write the introduction for the American edition of *Ariel* (1966). In it, he says: "everything in these poems is personal, confessional. She burns to be on the move, a walk, a ride, a journey, the flight of the queen bee."[23]

9. *Ariel: The Restored Edition. A Facsimile of Plath's Manuscript, Reinstating Her Original Selection and Arrangement.* Foreword by Frieda Hughes. London: Faber and Faber, 2004. First edition, first printing.

Six years following Hughes's death, their daughter, Frieda Hughes, published a "restored edition" of *Ariel*, rearranging and reinstating the forty poems to mirror her mother's original schema, noting that these poems had been completed in mid-November 1962, shortly

before the family's return to London from Devon the following month. This restored edition concludes on a note of triumph sounded symbolically by the cycle of the bee poems, in which the narrator reclaims her autonomy as an independent woman. Before Plath died, she completed an additional nineteen poems; these were stacked neatly on her desk next to the spring binder.

They unintentionally provided Hughes with several options as he determined how to rearrange and revise the manuscript. An appendix reproduces in facsimile the original typed manuscript, beginning with the title page, *ARIEL and Other Poems by Sylvia Plath*, followed by each typed poem. A second appendix reprints eight working drafts in facsimile and two drafts and the typeset proof of the poem "Ariel," published by *The Observer* under the variant title, "The Horse." The dust jacket (as shown here) is illustrated with an early draft of the title page, marked with three discarded titles written in Plath's hand: "The Rabbit Catcher" and "A Birthday Present" (each crossed-out), and in capital letters "DADDY." The title poem, "Ariel," completed on her thirtieth birthday, October 27, 1962, has been interpreted as her celebratory work, envisioning herself as "God's lioness" astride her horse named Ariel,

> I
> am the arrow . . .
>
> The dew that flies
> Suicidal, at one with the drive
> Into the red
> Eye, the cauldron of morning.
> (Plath, "Ariel")

Plath had taken up horseback riding in Devon and wrote in a draft for a BBC reading of this poem that "Ariel" was "another horseback riding poem . . . after a horse I'm especially fond of."[24]

10. *Sylvia Plath Collected Poems.* Edited by Ted Hughes. London: Faber and Faber, 1981. First edition, first impression. Inscribed "For Eric with love from Ted, 7th May 1982." The recipient was Eric Walter White, author, critic, and friend of Hughes. Winner of the 1982 Pulitzer Prize for poetry.

As Sylvia's fame spread among feminists and the literati, Hughes, who was her executor (Plath died intestate), was criticized for withholding some of her work from publication. And thus, in 1981, sixteen years after the publication of *Ariel*, Hughes published a more comprehensive edition of her poetry. Writing in the *Paris Review*, Hughes justified his actions as an effort to display the range of her work in the best light. In his introduction to this edition, Hughes noted that Plath made chronological lists of her work, and that in 1960, she began dating the final typescript of each poem. He provided a numbered sequence of 224 poems written by Plath after 1955 and selected another fifty poems from her pre-1956 work for an appendix entitled "Juvenilia." (Writing to her brother Warren in July 1958, Plath had identified her poems written prior to 1956 as "juvenilia" [LH, 347].) Critics have noted errors in Hughes's chronology, citing sources that he may not have had access to at the time. Nancy Hargrove has proposed "reordered chronologies" of Plath's poems for the years 1956 through 1959, utilizing two of Plath's Cambridge Pocket Diaries that contain handwritten records for 1955–57, the Cambridge manuscript submitted in partial fulfillment of her Cambridge Tripos examination, and related archival material.[25] Once again, Hughes ended this collection with "Edge," a poem that critics characterized as a retelling of the Medea story, which he first used to conclude his edition of *Ariel* (1965). It begins:

> The woman is perfected. Her dead
> Body wears the smile of accomplishment.
> (Plath, "Edge")

11. "Go Get the Goodly Squab." Two undated typescript drafts with manuscript annotations.

These typescripts illustrate the development of a poem from a class assignment, with the professor's penciled comment (and the grade of A-), to a revised version of six quatrains with the heading "Sold to Harper's – April 1953." Published in *Harper's* (November 1954), Plath characterized this sale as her first professional acceptance as a poet. *Harper's* also bought "Doomsday" and "To Eva Descending the Stair." Plath's instructor, Alfred Fisher, penciled comments on her first draft: "fine work in sound," "sharp visual imagery," importance of "final polishing." The second draft shows Plath's manuscript revisions. When she returned to Smith in February 1954, Fisher offered her a weekly tutorial in poetics, which she accepted gratefully as "a signal honor" (LH, 149). Plath had published poems and stories between 1950 and 1953 in *Seventeen* and *Mademoiselle*, but considered significant the prospect of being published by *Harper's* magazine. She wrote in her journal, "Listen and shut up, oh, ye of little faith . . . something did happen. Russell Lynes of Harper's bought 3 poems for $100. Signifying what? First real professional acceptance, God, and all the possibilities: to keep cracking open my mind and my vocabulary" (UJ, 179). Editor Russell Lynes wrote to her that since they couldn't decide which one they liked best they were buying all three poems, reflecting not "weak-mindedness on our part but real enthusiasm."[26]

12. Ted Hughes. *The Hawk in the Rain.* New York: Harper & Brothers, 1957. First edition.

This text reflects on the symbiotic relationship and creative partnership shared by Plath and Hughes. Plath enthusiastically selected and typed her husband's poems on her newly purchased Olivetti, submitting this manuscript of forty poems to the New York-based Poetry Center's "First Publication" contest. This fateful action set Hughes on an irrevocable path to his eventual career as a poet, opening the door to his acceptance by British intellectuals. On February 22, 1957, he received a telegram from *Harper's* in New York, telling him that the judges—W. H. Auden, Stephen Spender, and Marianne Moore—who, Plath wrote to her mother, were "the three best practicing poets in the world today," had awarded Hughes its publication prize and that she had "worked so closely on these poems of Ted's and typed them so many countless times through revision after revision that I feel ecstatic about it all" (LH, 297).

One week earlier, Plath told her mother that she had submitted her own book of poems (now titled "*Two Lovers and a Beachcomber*") in February 1957 to the Yale Younger Poets Series. It did not win the competition, as she had hoped, and the loss was a source of disappointment, especially since her contemporary, Adrienne Rich, had won that contest as a Radcliffe undergraduate. However, Plath did submit a different version, sometimes referred to as "the Cambridge manuscript, a collection of forty-three poems submitted in partial fulfillment of the Cambridge Tripos" in May 1957.[27] Both of these book-length manuscripts pre-date *The Colossus* by almost three years.

13. *Saint Botolph's Review.* Edited by David Ross. Cambridge, 1956. Dark red stiff paper cover with tan dust jacket.

Contributors included Ted Hughes, Lucas Myers, and their circle of friends. The magazine was named after the rectory outside college limits, where a small number of undergraduates associated with Cambridge University had rooms. Three of Hughes's poems— "Fallgrief's Girlfriends" and two untitled poems—were included in the only issue of the magazine (pp. 16–19) and it was at the launch on February 26, 1956 that Plath and Hughes first met. (A fiftieth-anniversary issue was published in 2006.)

14. Ted Hughes. *Birthday Letters.* London: Faber and Faber, 1998. No. 143 of 300 copies, Dark blue cloth binding, gilt-stamped title on spine. Signed by the author.

Written over a period of twenty-five years, and published nine months before his death in October 1998, these eighty-eight poems are the only direct, personal statement that Hughes has made about his life with Sylvia. They constitute a striking memorial to Plath, her poetry, and their lives together. He begins the text with the poem, "Fulbright Scholars," which reminisces about Plath's arrival in Cambridge as he views her photo in a news report, describing "her long hair, loose waves, Veronica Lake bang," her "exaggerated American grin for the cameras."[28] Alluding to T. S. Eliot's poem, "The Love Song of J. Alfred Prufrock," he asks, "Was it then I bought a peach?" In the poems that follow, he remembers shared moments together—gestures, conversations, and events in their lives—their children, travels, creative collaboration, painful separation, and her suicide. Further evidence of the text's fugue-like cadence and structure occurs in his final poem, "Red," recalling Plath's poem, "Kindness," and its oft-quoted phrase, "The blood jet is poetry." His closing poem in this text begins:

> Red was your color
> If not red, then white
> But red was what you wrapped around you
> Blood-red. Was it blood?
> (Hughes, "Red")

These lines recall her journal description of their first meeting at the launch party for *Saint Botolph's Review* (cat. 13). Plath wore a red hair band, which he "ripped" from her head, "And when he kissed my neck I bit him long and hard on the cheek" until "blood was running down his face" (UJ, 212).

36

III. Getting into Print: Periodicals, Magazines and Ephemera

This section focuses on periodicals and magazines of the '50s and '60s that served as outlets for Plath's poems and stories. She was methodical and determined to get into print, partly as a means of earning additional income but primarily for the recognition she gained from her peers and from poetry and fiction editors in her quest to be known as a serious writer. As she confided to her journal, "I have written lines that qualify me to be The Poetess of America (as Ted will be The Poet of England and her dominions)" (UJ, 360). One has to admire the persistence of her efforts and the systematic ways in which she steadily built her record of acceptances, prizes, and awards in college, graduate school, and as a wife and mother.

For the past ten years, I have been augmenting my Plath collection with periodicals and related ephemera in which she published her work. Plath kept up a steady flow of poetry submissions to both British and American publications, maintaining both typed and handwritten records of submissions, acceptances, and rejections. She could not have known, however, that her work would be critiqued and analyzed continuously after she died, becoming part of her biography as critics sought to define her genius, her identity, and her legacy. The materials here set out a chronology of what she and others considered "breakthroughs" in her literary career. Plath was tenacious in her efforts to get into print in a national magazine; her first appearance occurred in 1950 with the publication in *Seventeen* of her short story, "And Summer Will Not Come Again" (August) and her poem, "Ode to a Bitten Plum" (November). Other turning points occurred with the purchase of three poems by *Harper's* in 1953, an acceptance by *The New Yorker* in 1958; her editing of "new" American poets in the *Critical Quarterly Poetry Supplement* in 1961, and her lifetime and posthumous contributions to *Atlantic Monthly, Encounter, Gemini, London, Poetry* and other American and British periodicals.

15. *Seventeen* magazine, with "Den of Lions", May 1951, pp. 127, 144–45.

Plath muses in her journal about leaving her home in Wellesley to begin her first semester at college: on her desk at home is the manuscript of "Den of Lions," which she proclaims is "the best story I've ever written" (UJ, 22). She had entered it in a contest sponsored by *Seventeen*, winning third prize, and writes: "How can I tell Bob [the boyfriend she will leave behind] that my happiness streams from having wrenched a piece out of my life, a piece of hurt and beauty, and transformed it to typewritten words on paper?" (UJ, 22). As became evident in her journals and her poetry and prose, Plath made frequent use of her interactions and her experiences throughout her life.

16. *Mademoiselle* magazine, with "Sunday at the Mintons'," August 1952, pp. 255, 371–78.

In her sophomore year at Smith College, Plath won *Mademoiselle* magazine's fiction-writing contest and a prize of $500 for this story, published in the annual College Board issue. This magazine, published for sixty-six years by Street and Smith (1935–1961), and then by Condé Nast (1962–2001), boasted a readership of 1.1 million at the time of its closing.[29] It catered initially to "smart, young women" in the "18-to-30 age group above average in education and taste," thriving for many years in a lucrative advertising environment. In the '50s and '60s, the magazine cultivated its relationship with female college students through an annual competition, selecting from among the winners, twenty guest editors and up to fifty runners-up for its national advisory board. The guest editors participated in the production of the 400-page college issue published each August. Class divisions were still evident in the early '50s; as a scholarship student at an elite women's college, Plath viewed a guest editorship at *Mademoiselle* as her entrée into popular journalism while continuing to hone her literary talents. In the short term, the prize money would also be useful for acquiring and accessorizing a suitable wardrobe. Women's fashion magazine publishing was one of the few fields open to young women in postwar America, and in December 1952, Plath learned that she was one of 750 College Board members selected from nearly 2000 applicants to compete in the three-part competition. As the winner of a guest editorship in 1953, Plath became disillusioned about the life of a career woman at a prominent fashion magazine in New York City, incorporating some of her encounters at *Mademoiselle* into the opening chapters of her novel, *The Bell Jar* (cat. 49). Artifacts in my collection provide a personal glimpse from my memory bank, and my fleeting connection with Sylvia Plath outside the classroom.

17. Greeting card from Sylvia Plath to her mother, Aurelia Schober Plath, Friday, 24 April 1953, inscribed "Much love to/my favorite mummy! /your/Sivvy/." Card opening to one-page typed letter addressed "Dear mother..."

This letter is illustrative of the newsy and detailed communications that Plath frequently sent to her mother, letters that she addressed formally, "Dear mother," but signed with her mother's nickname for her—"Sivvy." Of particular interest are her comments about her pending scholarship application for Frank O'Connor's creative writing course at Harvard Summer School, her continuous money problems, her skepticism about her chances of winning a guest editorship, and her meeting W. H. Auden, "the most delightfully brilliant man," who was then a visiting professor at Smith. The denial of a scholarship to take O'Connor's course that summer is thought to have contributed to her depression.

18. Letter from Marybeth Little, College Board editor, *Mademoiselle*, to "Dear College Board Member," dated May 20, 1953.

I was also interested in journalism and a job at a high-profile fashion magazine, and competed for selection as a guest editor. The contest involved submitting an initial essay in fall 1952, followed by three assignments in winter/spring 1953. It also involved an assessment of a candidate's academic record, work experience, publication history, and other less tangible factors. In April 1953, Plath and I were invited to meet with *Mademoiselle's* College Board editor, Miss Marybeth Little, who was coming up to Northampton for an arts conference. The three of us sat together during the weekly chapel, Miss Little seated between Sylvia and me. She complimented me on my essays, indicating that Sylvia would be chosen as guest editor. I subsequently received this two-page letter on peach stationery notifying me of my appointment to the *Mademoiselle* national College Board, one of "fifty finalists who were runners-up"; ten of us were then enrolled at Smith.

19. *The Atlantic Monthly,* with "Circus in Three Rings," vol. 196, August 1955, p. 68.

One of the first periodicals to publish Plath's poems and stories, demonstrating the literary character of magazines in the post-World War II years. Although its major focus was on current affairs, the editors incorporated poetry, fiction, and arts reviews into each issue. In an introduction to its poetry section, the editor noted that they receive "as many as 1500 poems a month" and in the interest of encouraging "those writers as yet unestablished, we shall from time to time devote a number of pages to the work of young poets."[30] Plath's poem, "Circus in Three Rings," appeared in this issue. A manuscript book collection titled "Circus and Three Rings," assembled by Plath "towards the end of her senior year at Smith College in May/June 1955," was compiled for a course in poetic composition, according to Steinberg, who provides the manuscript's table of contents on his blog.[31]

20. *delta*, with "Winter Words," vol. 9, Summer 1956, pp. 5, 6.

One of many "little" magazines with a university constituency, *delta* was published from 1953 to 1981 at Cambridge University. Plath became part of the Cambridge literary scene as an American Fulbright scholar; she published in its journals, dated its editor, Christopher Levenson, and met Hughes at a student party.

21. *Gemini*, with "Spinster" and "Vanity Fair," vol. 1, Spring 1957, pp. 6–8.

The lead editorial in the inaugural issue of this Oxford and Cambridge poetry journal stated its purpose: "to avoid the parochialism of a single university and to publish the best work of senior as well as junior members of both . . . bring[ing] young writers to the attention of older ones" and "showing other standards than the academic."[32] Two of Plath's poems followed an introduction by Stephen Spender, again showing that she was part of the university's literary scene.

22. *Poetry*, with "Wreath for a Bridal" and five other poems, vol. 89, January 1957, pp. 231–37.

On October 2, 1956, Plath learned that six of her poems would be published by this major American journal, prompting Hughes to write from his parents' house in Yorkshire: "Now you are set, I never read six poems of anyone all together in *Poetry*. It will spellbind every American Editor," and shows that your poems are "eminently salable."[33] His expression of support for her as a poet was important to Plath in the early days of their marriage, signaling that the creative partnership she sought as a writer rather than a muse was within her grasp. She wrote in her journal: "there are no rules for this kind of wifeliness—I must make them up as I go along and will do so" (UJ, 412).

23. *The New Yorker*, with "Mussel Hunter at Rock Harbor," August 9, 1958, p. 22.

A major breakthrough for Plath occurred when *The New Yorker* accepted this 91-line poem in June 1958. In his letter to Plath, Howard Moss, the magazine's poetry editor, wrote: "seems to me a marvelous poem & I'm happy to say we're taking it for *The New Yorker* ..." (UJ, 397). She had written this poem based on experiences during an afternoon in the summer of 1957, when she and Hughes hunted for mussels to use as fish-bait in a shallow harbor with rock pools during their seven-week summer vacation on Cape Cod. More acceptances followed from this magazine, and in March 1961, while she was in the hospital following an appendectomy, Hughes brought her an airmail letter from *The New Yorker,* offering her a one-year renewable "first reading" contract, signified by a higher pay rate per poem and a cost-of-living bonus.

24. *The Grecourt Review,* with "Sculptor" To Leonard Baskin, vol. 11, no. 4, May 1959, p. 282. Edited and published four times a year by the students, independently, at Smith College, Northampton, MA.

Plath dedicated this poem as a tribute to Leonard Baskin, sculptor, printmaker, and a faculty member of the Art Department at Smith College from 1953 to 1974. They met when Plath was teaching in the English Department. In the years that followed, Hughes and Baskin forged a close friendship as well as a working relationship. Hughes wrote that "Leonard Baskin's work struck her [Sylvia] very hard, as well it might, since some of the gods he was carving at the time were also part of her pantheon...."[34] "Sculptor" appears in both the American and British editions of *The Colossus and Other Poems* (1960, 1962). Baskin also played a significant role in the development of the Rainbow Press in the 1970s, designing its colophon and illustrating a number of its imprints, including two of Plath's books: *Pursuit* (1971) and *Dialogue Over a Ouija Board* (1981).

25. *Critical Quarterly Supplement Number 2*, "American Poetry Now," Sylvia Plath, ed., 1961.

SELECTIONS FROM CAT. 19–33.

In her brief introduction, Plath states she selected twenty-six poems by "new and/or youngish American poets for the most part unknown in Britain."[35] Poems by Denise Levertov, W. S. Merwin, Howard Nemerov, Adrienne Rich, George Starbuck, and Richard Wilbur appear in this issue.

26. *Poetry at the Mermaid.* Souvenir program of Poetry Festival, July 16–23, 1961, sponsored by the Poetry Book Society and the Arts Council of Great Britain, John Wain, director.

On July 17, Plath, one of eight poets whose work was commissioned "by Messrs. Guinness to write poems of between 50 and 200 lines," read her now-famous poem "Tulips." The event was originally recorded by the BBC; in 2010, the British Library Board released *The Spoken Word: Sylvia Plath*, a compilation of conversations, talks, and readings by Plath as a 70-minute CD.

27. *London Magazine*, with "Six Poems," vol. 1, Aug. 1961, pp. 5–10.

Following publication of *The Colossus* (1960), Plath gained greater prominence in the British literary world. Six of her poems lead off in the first volume of this reconstituted version of the monthly periodical. Edited by the poet and critic Alan Ross from 1961 until his death in 2001, it was an important outlet for international writers. This issue also features works in translation by Bertolt Brecht, Paul Klee, and Ossip Mandelshtam.

28. *Encounter,* with "Death & Co," "Lady Lazarus," "Daddy," and seven other poems, vol. XXI, October 1963, pp. 45–65.

Ten of Plath's poems, all written in 1962 and published posthumously with a brief introduction by Hughes, who commented on the "intensity of her spirits" and the "uncompromising thoroughness" of her language. Plath had published "The Colossus" in an earlier issue of *Encounter* (April 1962). This Anglo-American intellectual and cultural journal was founded in 1953 by poet Stephen Spender and journalist Irving Kristol and published in London. Unbeknownst to many contributors, it was partly funded by the US Central Intelligence Agency in the '60s, prompting some literary figures to withdraw their support following disclosure of those revelations in 1967.

29. *The Review,* vol. 9, October 1963.

A magazine of poetry and criticism published by the Oxonian Press in Oxford, with "The Last Poems of Sylvia Plath" and "Sylvia Plath," an essay by A. Alvarez (pp. 20–26), edited from his talk written for the BBC Third Programme. This issue has a cover photograph of Plath.

30. *Observer Weekend Review,* with "A Poet's Epitaph" by A. Alvarez, Poetry Editor, February 17, 1963, p. 23.

Six days following Plath's suicide, her close friend, A. Alvarez, wrote a memorial essay and published four of her last poems: "Edge," "Kindness," "The Fearful" and "Contusion." The epitaph states, in part,

> In these last poems, she was systematically probing that narrow, violent area … between experience which can be transmuted into poetry and that which is overwhelming. It represents a totally new breakthrough in modern verse, and establishes her, I think, as the most gifted woman poet of our time.[36]

This issue of the *Weekend Review* featured writings by two notable women with international reputations based on their recent scholarship: Simone de Beauvoir, author of *The Second Sex*, and Rachel Carson, author of *Silent Spring*, with whom Plath was familiar.

31. *Critical Quarterly Poetry Supplement Number 6*, "American Poetry 1965" issue.

The second issue of this supplement features the work of American poets selected by Rella Lossy, and includes two of Plath's poems, "The Bee Meeting" and "Lady Lazarus." Poems by Robert Lowell, Anne Sexton, James Dickey, William Stafford, Adrienne Rich, and Theodore Roethke also appear.

32. *Tri-Quarterly*, "Womanly Issue: The Art of Sylvia Plath," no. 7, Fall 1966, pp. 11–101.

This special issue of a journal published by Northwestern University and edited by Charles Newman contains eighteen poems by Plath, all previously collected (pp. 11–38) and selected poems and essays on her work by A. Alvarez, Lois Ames, A. E. Dyson, Ted Hughes, Charles Newman and Anne Sexton (pp. 39–101).

33. *Ms. The New Magazine for Women*, "Three Women: A Play for Three Voices." Preview issue, January 1972: 85–88.

A departure from the traditional women's magazines that Plath had aspired to write for, *Ms.* focused national attention on the advancement of women's rights and their active participation in contemporary society. For this preview issue, the editors chose Plath's verse play, *Three Women*, in which three women in a hospital maternity ward meditate on childbirth and motherhood. A postscript comments that "poems written before her death in 1963 have made her a heroine, almost a cult figure, to millions of women."[37] Gloria Steinem and Dorothy Pitman Hughes founded *Ms.* magazine, with initial funding from *New York* magazine.

IV. Fine-Press and Small-Press Editions

Fine-press books unite many elements of the graphic arts: layout, design, illustration, typography, fine paper, language, and printing. Ted Hughes sought to integrate these components when he and his sister, Olwyn Hughes, founded the Rainbow Press in 1971, publishing works by Plath, his own work, and other poets in their cultural circle. While they worked together in selecting poets and texts for publication, Olwyn handled the finances and management of the press, and in 1981, they decided to cease operations. More than half of the sixteen titles produced between 1971 and 1981 were printed at The Rampant Lions Press in Cambridge by Sebastian and Will Carter, a small publisher of fine editions and a printer for other publishers. In this section, I describe fine-press and small-press editions, all of which were printed at private presses in limited editions. Four of Plath's works were published with the Rainbow Press imprint: *Crystal Gazer, Lyonnesse, Pursuit,* and *Dialogue Over a Ouija Board.* Small-press editions commissioned by Hughes contained minimal content, in some cases a single unillustrated poem. In addition to the Rainbow Press imprint, Hughes granted permission to Embers Handpress, Rougemont Press, Sceptre Press, and Anvil Press Poetry to publish limited editions of selected poems and stories, both his own and Plath's.

34. *Crystal Gazer and Other Poems.* Illustration by Sylvia Plath. London: Rainbow Press, 1971. Two editions: (1) Designed by Juliet Standing and printed at the Daedalus Press in Stoke Ferry, Norfolk on J. Barcham Green dampened hand-made paper, Hayle Mill, Maidstone, Kent.; bound by Zaehnsdorf in quarter buckram, hand-made Japanese paper sides, black paper-covered slipcase; no. 386 of 400 copies;

(2) full Kelmscott-style vellum binding by Zaehnsdorf with red silk ties, housed in a later red silk solander box lined with Japanese paper; 1 of 20 copies; marked "out of series."

This volume contains twenty-three previously uncollected poems composed by Plath between 1951 and 1962; many appeared here for the first time.[38] "Crystal Gazer," the title poem, written in June 1956 at the time of their marriage, tells of a bride and groom who ask Gerd, a fortune-teller, to foretell their fate; it illustrates the intensity of Plath's imagery about love and death in her early work. Other poems selected for this inaugural publication by Rainbow Press include three written by Plath as an undergraduate: "Mad Girl's Love Song," a villanelle that appeared in *Mademoiselle* magazine in 1953; "Go Get the Goodly Squab," also written in 1953, in this case as a class assignment and published by *Harper's* magazine (cat. 11); and "Circus in Three Rings" (cat. 19), the title poem of a manuscript that she assembled for a special studies course in May/June 1955. The illustration by Plath is a reproduction of an undated line drawing of a corn vase held by a peasant girl in costume, balancing a wicker basket on her shoulder. Plath had seen the vase in the mobile home of family friends, the Spaldings, who she visited during her Cape Cod vacation with Hughes in July 1957, drawing a sketch and writing notes in her journal for a story that she called "Mama McFague and the Corn Vase Girl" (UJ, 615).

35. *Lyonnesse. Poems by Sylvia Plath.* London: Rainbow Press, 1971. First edition. Printed by the Rampant Lions Press, Cambridge. Bound by Zaehnsdorf in full sepia calf, with title blocked on spine in gilt; ochre cloth slipcase. No. 81 of 90 copies.

This slim volume contains twenty-one of Plath's previously uncollected poems. Facsimiles of two drafts written on Smith College memorandum paper and slightly enlarged, form the end-papers in this edition. The title poem, "Lyonnesse" (1962), concludes the volume.

36. *Pursuit.* London: Rainbow Press, 1973 [i.e., 1974]. First edition. With an etching and five drawings by Leonard Baskin; book design and hand-lettered title page also by Baskin. Signed and numbered black-and-white etching by Baskin laid in. No. 52 of 100 copies hand-set in Centaur type at the Daedalus Press, Norfolk; printed by Will and Sebastian Carter at the Rampant Lions Press, Cambridge; black leather binding by Zaehnsdorf.

Seated at her desk in her Cambridge dormitory room, Plath wrote the title poem following her first meeting with Hughes, remarking in her journal: "Wrote a full-page poem about the dark forces of lust: 'pursuit.' It is not bad. It is dedicated to Ted Hughes" (UJ, 214). She took as its

epigraph a line from Racine's *Phaedre*, a play she was studying at the time, "Dans le fond des forêts votre image me suit." ("In the depths of the forest, your image pursues me.")[39] Plath sent a draft of this poem to her mother, declaring that it was influenced "a bit by Blake," was "more powerful than any of my other 'metaphysical' poems," and should be read "slowly and deliberately aloud" (LH, 222).

37. *Dialogue Over a Ouija Board.* Cambridge: Rainbow Press, 1981. Drawing and colophon by Leonard Baskin; designed and

CAT. 37. By permission of the Estate of Leonard Baskin. © Estate of Leonard Baskin. Courtesy Galerie St. Etienne, New York.

printed by Sebastian Carter. No. 130 of 140 copies. In cardboard slipcase covered in light brown hand-made Japanese paper.

A verse dialogue written by Plath in 1957. Hughes stated that she derived the dialogue from "the actual spirit text" of one of their Ouija sessions with their "favorite spirit," the Greek god Pan. In Plath's exploration of mysticism through verse dialogue, her "stand-ins," Sybil and Leroy, await the presence of Pan, who speaks to them in capital letters, interrupting their verse, and controlling their movements on the Ouija board. In her poem "Metamorphosis," later retitled "Faun," she thought of Hughes as Pan,[40] writing to her mother about a night "we went into the moonlight to find owls" (LH, 234). Baskin's drawing of a faun's head is meant to embody Pan as shown in *Pursuit* (cat. 36). Hughes introduced Plath to the study of astrology and the occult, and in her journals, she wrote of learning how to read her astrological signs and engaging in "a self-hypnotic state of boldness and vigor" as a means of enhancing her creativity (UJ, 518). Shortly after meeting Plath, Hughes had written to his sister that: "She is Scorpio Oct 27th, moon in Libra, last degrees of Aries rising and has her Mars smack on my sun, which is all very appropriate."[41]

38. *Fiesta Melons.* Introduction by Ted Hughes. Exeter: The Rougemont Press, 1971. Designed and printed by Eric Cleave and hand bound by Alan Constance. No. 88 of 150 copies.

Plath produced the ten poems and fourteen pen-and-ink drawings contained in this charming volume. Her poem and drawings for "Southern Sunrise" describe the small Spanish fishing village of Benidorm on the Mediterranean Sea, where Plath and Hughes spent seven idyllic weeks on their honeymoon from July 7–August 20, 1956. Plath has sketched the cottages facing the sea, describing the "quartz-clear dawn" and "the blue drench of Angels' Bay," out of which "Rises the round red watermelon sun."

Colour of lemon, mango, peach,
These storybook villas
Still dream behind
Shutters, their balconies
Fine as hand—
Made lace, or a leaf-and-flower pensketch.

Tilting with the winds,
On arrowy stems,
Pineapple-barked,
A green crescent of palms
Send up its forked
Firework of fronds.

A quartz-clear dawn
Inch by bright inch
Gilds all our Avenue,
And out of the blue drench
Of Angels' Bay
Rises the round red watermelon sun.

Plaster tenements, Benidorm, Spain

Palms and pueblos, Benidorm

39. *A Day in June. A Short Story by Sylvia Plath.* Ely: Embers Handpress, 1981. First edition. No. 112 of 160 copies printed on Barcham Green hand-made papers; grey cover handmade in the Auvergne by Richard de Bas; text hand-set in Monotype Garamond and printed at the Fish Inn, Sutton Gault, Ely. Finished on May 9, 1981.

This story had been published in the first paperback edition of *Johnny Panic and the Bible of Dreams* (Faber and Faber, 1979).

40. *The Green Rock.* Ely: Embers Handpress, 1982. First edition. No. 34 of 160 copies hand-printed on various Barcham Green hand-made papers and covered in pale green Auvergne paper. Presswork concluded on June 11, 1982.

This story was written in winter 1949 and also published in the first paperback edition of *Johnny Panic and the Bible of Dreams* (1979).

SELECTIONS FROM CAT. 39–46.

41. *Million Dollar Month.* Farnham, Surrey: Sceptre Press, 1971. First edition. No. 112 of 150 copies printed on laid paper.

A previously unpublished poem. Sceptre Press was founded by Martin Booth; it operated from 1969–1981.

42. *Two Poems.* ["Incommunicado" (1956) and "Firesong" (1958).] Knotting, Bedfordshire: Sceptre Press, 1980. First edition. No. 6 of 300 copies, "the first 75 of which are especial." Printed in monotype Baskerville on Zerkall Rauh paper and hand-sewn at Skelton's Press, Wellingborough; in medium brown wrappers.

Both poems were included by Hughes in *Collected Poems* (1981).

43. *Wreath for a Bridal.* Farnham, Surrey: Sceptre Press, 1970. First edition. No 64 of 100 copies printed on Glastonbury laid paper. Single poem.

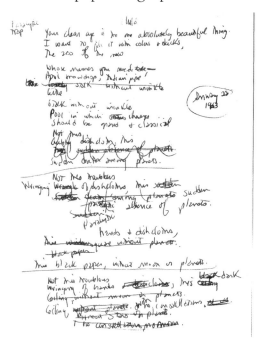

CHILD

Your clear eye is the one absolutely beautiful thing.
I want to fill it with colours and ducks,
The zoo of the new

Whose names you meditate -
April snowdrop, Indian pipe,
Little

Stalk without wrinkle,
Pool in which images
Should be grand and classical

Not this troublous
Wringing of hands, this dark
Ceiling without a star.

Written by Plath in May 1956, one month before their marriage, Hughes included "Wreath for a Bridal" as the first poem in the British edition of *Winter Trees* (1971) and in *Lyonnesse*.

44. *Child.* Exeter: Rougemont Press, 1971. First edition. No. 173 of 325 copies. Single poem. Designed and printed by Eric Cleave. Facsimile of Plath's manuscript draft, side by side with the printed poem. Sewn into stiff, greenish-blue wrappers. Also included in *Lyonnesse*.

45. *Two Uncollected Poems.* ["Dialogue Between Ghost and Priest" and "Child's Park Stones."] London: Anvil Press Poetry, 1980. First edition. No. 186 of 450 copies. Designed and printed by Ithaca Press, based in Greenwich, London.

    Peter Jay founded this press in 1968; it specializes in contemporary English poets, some Irish and American poets, and a range of translated poetry from ancient classics to modern and contemporary poets.

46. Anneke Brassinga (trans.). *Sylvia Plath: Blackberrying.* Uitgave: De Lange Afstand, 1984. Designed by Peter Yvon de Vries. Copy no. 7 on Velin d'Arches paper.

    This poem by Plath was written on September 23, 1961 and sold to *The New Yorker* that November. She wrote from Devon, asking her mother to tell Warren (her brother) that it was "about the day we all went blackberrying together down the land that sloped to the sea" (LH, 436). It was translated into Dutch by Brassinga; the original English version appears on the facing page.

v. Prose Writings

Sylvia Plath is best known as a poet and the author of *The Bell Jar*, her novel written under the pseudonym of Victoria Lucas. Her prose writings range from short stories, both published and unpublished, and essays, to her detailed journals as transcribed from the original manuscripts, to her equally expansive letters, a sample of which were included in a volume edited by her mother, Aurelia Plath.

47. *Johnny Panic and the Bible of Dreams and Other Prose Writings.* Edited by Ted Hughes. London: Faber and Faber, 1977.

48. *Johnny Panic and the Bible of Dreams: Short Stories, Prose, and Diary Excerpts.* Edited by Ted Hughes. New York: Harper & Row, 1979.

Plath began writing prose and, from an early age, to keep a handwritten diary or journal in which she wrote drafts of poems and recorded a variety of ideas, thoughts, and observations. Her storytelling began while she was in junior high school and, according to Hughes, "she declared her ambition" as an undergraduate to be a successful story writer, "of the high-power practical, popular American type...."[42] Most of the stories in the 1977 edition, selected for inclusion by Hughes and his sister, Olwyn, had been published in the 1960s, with the title story, *Johnny Panic and the Bible of Dreams,* having appeared in *Atlantic Monthly* in 1968. When Hughes learned that Aurelia Plath had sold her collection of Plath's manuscripts to the Lilly Library at Indiana University, and that the collection included about two hundred early poems, fifty-seven short stories (mostly unpublished), and fifteen short prose essays, he secured copies of this cache of manuscripts, and Faber and Faber published a selection in a paperback edition in 1979.

During this time, Hughes communicated with Frances Mc-Cullough, an editor at Harper & Row with whom he had worked previously. Olwyn Hughes collaborated with McCullough to produce an expanded American edition in 1979. It brought together twenty stories, five essays, and four notebook excerpts that, at the time, were not to be included in the first edition of Plath's journals (1982). They selected the stories from among seventy, mostly unpublished manuscripts. The title story, "Johnny Panic and the Bible of Dreams," was based on Sylvia's experience as a part-time records clerk at Massachusetts General Hospital during their sojourn in Boston in 1958. Some selections had appeared in magazines, for example, "Sunday at the Mintons'" (cat. 16), which had won first prize in the *Mademoiselle* fiction contest in 1952. Others were subsequently published as small-press editions, for example, *A Day in June* and *The Green Rock*.

The 1950s were a prosperous decade in magazine publishing, and advertising provided significant revenues to fill the coffers of slick publications. Plath was aware of the potential for remuneration as a contributor to these magazines and aspired to be a journalist as well as a creative writer. Her journal entries bear witness to this goal and contain observations and notes about people, places, and things for future reference in character and plot development. *The New Yorker* was a perennial candidate, but the *Ladies' Home Journal, Saturday Evening Post, McCall's, Good Housekeeping,* and *Woman's Day* also perked her interest. Many of the stories collected in *Johnny Panic and the Bible of Dreams* were previously featured in other publications, ranging from *Granta* to *Sewanee Review*.

While scholars and critics have long examined the biographical content in Plath's poetry and her novel *The Bell Jar*, the stories that comprise *Johnny Panic and the Bible of Dreams* show how Plath saw every experience as rich material for her craft. In a journal entry, Plath wrote herself a note: "Keep a notebook of physical events.

My visit to the tattoo shop and my job at the hospital provided me with two good stories" (UJ, 527). And to her mother, she wrote, "I will slave and slave until I break into those slicks" (LH, 290). In his introduction to this text, Hughes comments that the stories did not always meet Sylvia's high standards but, in his view, "they seem interesting enough to keep if only as notes toward her inner autobiography."[43] His sister, Olwyn, gave as a rationale for their selection the importance of preserving Sylvia's posthumous reputation. Both Ted and Olwyn Hughes were keenly aware of the growing interest in Plath, not only as a writer but also a cultural icon. Indeed, they sought to capitalize on her reputation in granting permission to publish her prose fiction.

49. Victoria Lucas (pseud.). *The Bell Jar.* London: Heinemann, 1963. First edition. One of 2000 copies.

The Bell Jar was Plath's only novel, published in England under the pseudonym Victoria Lucas on January 14, 1963, less than one month before her death. The bell jar symbolizes the heroine's entrapment by the conventions of mid-twentieth century mores that she asserts are threatening her creativity and growth as an autonomous woman and a poet. The novel's heroine, Esther Greenwood, is perceived as an autobiographical representation of the author, framed by her experiences as guest managing editor of *Mademoiselle* magazine in June 1953 and her descent into depression, followed by her suicide attempt in August 1953 and confinement in a psychiatric hospital in Belmont, Massachusetts. The novel attracted little notice, which greatly disappointed Plath. However, shortly after her suicide, A. Alvarez, poetry editor of *The Observer*, revealed Plath's identity as its author in a BBC broadcast in the fall of 1963. Hughes's London publisher, Faber and Faber, brought out an edition crediting Plath as the author in 1966. During the next five years, he sought its publication in the US despite objections raised by Aurelia Plath, who was

concerned about its portrayal of her and other individuals. A compromise agreement with Hughes was eventually reached, granting Sylvia's mother permission to publish an American edition of her daughter's letters to her (subsequently published in the US in 1975 as *Letters Home*). *The Bell Jar* has been in print continuously since 1963, and issued in numerous editions worldwide; it has also been translated into more than twenty languages, including Chinese, Hungarian, and Turkish. Shown here are four recent British, Danish, Chinese, and Italian editions. The soberly illustrated first edition published as the work of Victoria Lucas is shown under a bell jar.

50. *Above the Oxbow: Selected Writings of Sylvia Plath.* Engravings by Barry Moser. Northampton, MA: Catawba Press, 1985. First edition. With four original wood engravings, including one of Plath, by Barry Moser. No. 136 of 325 copies.

This slim volume contains writings completed in 1958, when Plath and Hughes lived in an apartment in Northampton, near Smith College, where she taught from 1957–58 as an instructor in the English Department. The title poem and story have as their locale Prospect House, once a tourist hotel on top of Skinner Mountain. The title poem begins:

> Here in this valley of discreet academies
> We have not mountains, but mounts, truncated hillocks
> To the Adirondacks, to northern Manado
> Themselves mere rocky hillocks to an Everest.
>
> (Plath, "Above the Oxbow")

51. "Mary Ventura and the Ninth Kingdom," carbon typescript, 22 pages. Revised version completed December 27, 1954. [AND:] Rejection letter from Margarita G. Smith, fiction editor, *Mademoiselle* magazine, dated March 11, 1953.

This typescript exemplifies Plath's working style while still an undergraduate, typing drafts of her stories and poems on her Royal portable (ubiquitous in the '50s), suitable for mailing to prospective magazine publishers and, more likely, for fulfilling course assignments. Plath wrote that this typescript was an experiment in "symbolic imagery," employing religious imagery in a secular context. Her mother had written a note on an earlier version that, in her view, it was "very symbolic of Sylvia's life," portraying Mary being coaxed on to a mysterious train by her parents, then pulling the emergency cord to escape from its eventual last stop at the "ninth kingdom."

Plath submitted this story to *Mademoiselle* in 1953; following its rejection by the magazine, she considered submitting a revised version to a national contest but decided it was too fanciful and set it aside. This story remains unpublished.

52. *Letters Home. Correspondence 1950–1963. Selected and Edited with Commentary by Aurelia Schober Plath.* New York: Harper & Row, 1975. Signed by the author. Presentation copy to Beth Gillis, January 18, 1978. On flyleaf: "I rejoice in the friendliness of this gathering (ref. program at Dover Town Library). Thank you. Aurelia Plath." With an autograph note from Aurelia Plath to Beth Gillis stating, in part: "I enjoyed sharing what is so precious to me in the way of memory and to have such a warm, appreciative audience was delightful and gift enough."

Publishing the letters that Sylvia wrote to her mother Aurelia between 1950 and 1963 proved to be a contentious process. In effect, Hughes "owned the literary rights" to the hundreds of letters Plath had written; as a consequence, he held "the right of final approval."[44] He exercised that right by deleting letters that he felt compromised the family's right to privacy. Following protracted negotiations between Hughes and Harper and Row, a "legally vetted version" was published in 1975.[45] Harper's editor, Frances McCullough, claimed that "perhaps a quarter [of the letters] appear in the book."[46] Also included were letters to Sylvia's brother, Warren, and to Olive Higgins Prouty. Despite its brevity, *Letters Home* added a personal dimension to a critical understanding of Plath and the optimistic voice and persona she used in writing to her mother about the minutiae of her everyday life, signing her letters with the affectionate nickname "Sivvy," and offered new insights into her development as a writer and a woman.

53. Karen V. Kukil (ed.). *The Journals of Sylvia Plath: 1950–1962. Transcribed from the Original Manuscripts at Smith College.* London: Faber and Faber, 2000.

54. Ted Hughes and Frances McCullough (eds.). *The Journals of Sylvia Plath, 1950–1962.* New York: Dial Press, 1982.

Sylvia Plath kept diaries and journals from the age of eleven until her death at thirty, recording her thoughts, feelings, experiences, and events in her daily life. They provide an unusually detailed portrait of the poet in all her guises, chronicling her development as a writer, her marriage to Ted Hughes, and the two years they spent teaching and writing in New England. In 1981, Hughes sold Plath's papers in his possession to her alma mater, Smith College. The agreement was that he would serve as consulting editor on their publication, and due to his reticence about making public any intimate details of their marriage, only a third of the material in the journals was published by Dial Press. In a brief foreword, he indicated that he had sealed two of these journals, and that an additional two journals, one of which covered the period from 1960 to 1962 and one written by Plath in the last few months of her life (when she had returned to London from Devon), were not included in the transfer. According to Hughes, one had "disappeared," and the other, "which contained entries to within three days of Plath's suicide," he destroyed (UJ, ix). This revelation created a public furor, and in 1998, shortly before he died, Hughes unsealed the two bound journals in the possession of Smith College. *The Journals* encompass her adult years, having been meticulously transcribed from twenty-three original handwritten and typed manuscripts; the unabridged edition published in 2000 includes, for the first time, the two journals that were unsealed in 1998. Illustrations include candid shots, studio portraits, and facsimile pages of manuscripts. Journal fragments from 1960 to 1962, when Plath and Hughes were living in London and Devon with their children prior to their breakup, complete this edition. What makes these journals so vibrant are the random thoughts she records, the drafts of poems, the ideas for new stories, her descriptions of people she meets, the dialogues she carries on with herself and others, her responses to a myriad of interactions and experiences. Unlike the upbeat letters to her mother, the journals reveal the ambivalence and complexity of her personal and professional interactions with others. "Oh, I bite, I bite on life like a sharp apple. . . . I will seek to progress to whip myself on, to more and more—to learning. Always" (UJ, 141).

VI. Literary Influences

From an early age, Plath was a voracious reader, according to her mother, her teachers, and her peers. Her journals and letters are replete with references to the poets and writers she most admired and who influenced her work. In her published journals that begin in summer 1950, prior to her matriculation at Smith College, she acknowledges her debt to many poets, essayists, and novelists whose work she studied. In that context, I have been privileged to browse through 162 volumes from Plath's personal library, held by the Mortimer Rare Book Room at Smith College. (Indiana University has 158 volumes and Emory has 60 volumes.) I have also spent many hours reading her notes and papers in the Plath archives at these libraries. There are undoubtedly many more than I can display in this exhibition but in this section, I have drawn on three examples from her personal library on loan from Smith College: D. H. Lawrence, Edith Sitwell, and Wallace Stevens. I also display four books of poems from my own collection: by Robert Lowell, Marianne Moore, Theodore Roethke, and Anne Sexton, all further examples of her literary influences.

55. D. H. Lawrence. "The Mess of Love," in *The Complete Poems of D. H. Lawrence, Vol. II.* Kingswood, Surrey: Windmill Press, 1957, p. 204.

LENDER: Mortimer Rare Book Room, Smith College

Hughes gave a three-volume set of Lawrence's works to Plath on February 10, 1960, the date she signed the contract with Heinemann for *The Colossus*. Lawrence was one of the poets she most admired and that she had studied in depth for her English examination at Cambridge. Here Plath has underlined and dated (October 22, 1962) one poem, "The Mess of Love;" its first lines: "We've made a great mess of love/Since we made an ideal of it."[47] The date was five days before her thirtieth birthday and the month in which Hughes left their home in Devon. During this month, Plath wrote many of the searing poems that would form the *Ariel* text (cat. 8).

56. Robert Lowell (1917–1977). *Life Studies: New Poems and an Autobiographical Fragment.* New York: Farrar, Straus & Cudahy, 1959.

In *Life Studies*, Lowell employs an autobiographical, confessional mode of poetry. Plath was in the vanguard of women poets who adopted this methodology, and publication of this book elicited several laudatory reviews from American and British literary critics. Writing in *The Nation*, M. L. Rosenthal, who first characterized Lowell's poetry as confessional, observed: "To build a great poem out of the predicament and horror of the lost Self has been the recurrent effort of the most ambitious poetry of the last century. It is too early to say whether *Life Studies* is great art. It is certainly major art."[48] Hughes invited Lowell to write the foreword to the American edition of Plath's *Ariel*. In it, Lowell gives his first impressions on meeting Plath:

> for a couple of months seven years ago, she used to drop in on my poetry seminar.... She was willowy, long-waisted, sharp-elbowed, nervous, giggly, gracious—a brilliant tense presence embarrassed by restraint. Her humility and willingness to accept what was admired seemed at times to give her an air of maddening docility that hid her unfashionable patience and boldness.[49]

57. Marianne Moore (1887–1972). *The Complete Poems of Marianne Moore.* New York: Macmillan and The Viking Press, 1967.

Plath admired Moore, referring to her at different times in her journals as "one of the three best living poets," an "ageing giantess of poetic letters," and "The American Lady of Letters." She met Moore for the first time in April 1955, six weeks before her graduation from Smith College. Moore was a judge for the Kathryn Glascock Poetry Prize, an intercollegiate competition held annually at Mt. Holyoke College. Plath dutifully bought her book and read it carefully, describing Moore to her mother as "in her late seventies and as vital and humorous as someone's fairy godmother incognito." Plath tied for first prize, receiving a check for $50, "plus a pleasant glow" (LH, 168, 171). Three years later, on a visit to New York City in June 1958, Plath and Hughes had tea with Moore at her home in Brooklyn. She wrote her mother that Moore served them "strawberries, sesame-seed biscuits and milk and talked a blue streak" (LH, 340). Following that meeting, Plath sent Moore carbon copies of several poems, requesting a letter of recommendation for the Eugene Saxton Fellowship for Young Writers. One month later, she was disappointed to receive a caustic letter declining to support her application. She recognized that Moore not only was critical of her poems but of the carbon copies on which they had been sent: "my great & stupid error," Plath wrote, "sending carbons to the American Lady of Letters" (LH, 406). Plath did not win the Saxton Fellowship that year, but did succeed on her second try in November 1961, for which she was awarded $2000.

58. Theodore Roethke (1908–1963). *Collected Poems.* Garden City: Doubleday & Company, 1964.

In a letter to her mother, Plath writes about meeting Roethke at a party, referring to him as "the American poet I admire next to Robert Lowell." She described him as a "big, blond, Swedish-looking man, much younger-seeming than his 52 years" and someone she hoped to see again (LH, 393). Echoes of Roethke's influence on Plath were commented on by Knopf's poetry editor in asking that her seven-part poem, "Poem for a Birthday," be deleted from the manuscript for an American edition of *The Colossus*. Plath demurred, and the last two parts of this poem were retained in the Knopf edition (cat. 2). In a letter to Anne Sexton, she acknowledged her debt to Roethke, saying how much she admired him. In a brief memoir about Plath, Sexton commented: "Poets will not only hide influences. They will bury them! And not that her lines reminded me of Roethke—but the openness to metaphor, the way they both have (and Sylvia more so in her last work) of jumping straight into their own image and then believing it."[50]

59. Anne Sexton (1928–1974). *All My Pretty Ones.* Boston: Houghton Mifflin Co., 1962.

Plath and Sexton met in spring 1959, when they both audited Robert Lowell's poetry seminar at Boston University. When Plath returned to England in late 1959, the two women continued to correspond. Plath thanked Sexton for sending her first book of poems, *To Bedlam and Part Way Back* (1960), with "the beautiful words of Lowell" on the cover and her favorite poems of Sexton's, including "Elegy in the Classroom."[51] When Plath received Sexton's second book of poems, *All My Pretty Ones*, she wrote again, commenting on "The Black Art" as a favorite.[52] Biographer Heather Clark has pointed out the influence of Sexton's poem, "Letter Written on a Ferry While Crossing Long Island Sound" on Plath's "Fever 103°," also noting that Plath's iconic poem "Daddy" was "heavily influenced" by an uncollected Sexton poem, "My Friend, My Friend."[53]

60. Edith Sitwell (1887–1964). *The Canticle of the Rose, Poems 1917–1949.* New York: Vanguard Press, 1949.

LENDER: Mortimer Rare Book Room, Smith College

In drafting a list of outstanding living women poets, Plath cited "Edith Sitwell & Marianne Moore, the ageing giantesses & poetic grandmothers" (UJ, 360). She had read Sitwell as an undergraduate, and in a thirty-page paper, had traced her development as a poet, "through her first bucolic Eden, her rocketing jazz fantasies, her nightmare cannibal land, her wanton hell of the cold, and her metaphysical sun-permeated universe."[54] Plath was moved by Sitwell's early poems, in which the "subtleties of sound textures" and "fusion of the senses" gave the reader a "heightened consciousness of life."[55] In Plath's poem, "Alicante Lullaby," she replicates the "cacophony" of stimuli that assault her senses during her summer in southern Spain, building to a crescendo of sound from booming loudspeakers, and with her head "on the pillow," becoming a lullaby of "susurrous lyres and viols."[56]

61. Wallace Stevens (1879–1955). *The Collected Poems.* New York: Alfred A. Knopf, 1955.

LENDER: Mortimer Rare Book Room, Smith College

Plath's copy of this text, borrowed from her undergraduate library, contains many underlined and starred passages about the imagination and its relationship to the real world. In an interview with Ekbert Faas, professor of humanities at York University in Toronto, Hughes commented that Stevens was "a kind of god to her.... Her early poetry is Wallace Stevens in almost every other line."[57] In his thoughtful analysis of Stevens's influence on Plath's early poetry, the late Leonard Scigaj, another Hughes scholar, concluded that, through immersing herself in Stevens as an undergraduate, Plath was

> developing far deeper and more pervasive roots than other important influences: the technical brilliance of Auden, the sonorous voice of Dylan Thomas, the daringly swift and acute observations of Marianne Moore, the studied ambiguities of [John Crowe] Ransom, or the nursery rhyme psychic minimalism of Roethke.[58]

In March 1958, Plath wrote in her journal that she would be submitting a poem of the required 350 lines to a Wallace Stevens Poetry Contest, incorporating "10 small poems into one large one provisionally titled, 'Mules That Angels Ride ...'" (UJ, 350). Two weeks later, she noted that she "sent off a group of eight poems, seven of them new, under the title 'Mules That Angels Ride...' to a Wallace Stevens Contest" (UJ, 357). The contest, with a cash prize of $1,000, was sponsored by Southern Florida College in Lakeland, Florida. Plath wanted this group of eight poems to be "about the spirit, luminous, making itself manifest in art, house, trees and faces" (UJ, 352). She took the title from a line in part VII of Stevens's comic poem, "Le Monocle de Mon Oncle," in which the narrator, a poet, "delivers an extended, flamboyantly embellished, monologue to love in all its evocations."[59] Plath's entry did not win this contest, and it is not known whether this particular draft, perhaps renamed, is still extant.[60]

VII. Contemporary Adaptations

In collecting Plath's works, I have been intrigued with varied interpretations of her work by her contemporaries in the literary world and in allied artistic professions. Examples of these works exhibited range from poetic interpretations and novels to musical compositions, theatrical productions and artistic interpretations and tributes.

GRAPHIC ARTS

62. Jim Dine (b. 1935). *The Temple of Flora*. San Francisco: Arion Press, 1984. Twenty-eight drypoint engravings with botanical notes compiled and poetry selected by Glenn Todd & Nancy Dine, executed at the Atelier Crommelynck and printed by Robert E. Townsend in Georgetown, MA, each measuring 18 x 12" on a 20½ x 14" page. Text printed letterpress from handset Monotype Romulus type; bound in quarter dark-green goatskin with olive-grey cloth over boards; housed in an olive-grey cloth box with a relief sculpture by Dine on the lid, representing Flora's temple gate. Signed and numbered by the artist.

Artist Jim Dine designed this folio as a contemporary interpretation of Robert John Thornton's *The Temple of Flora* (1807) in scale and scheme of presentation. Working directly on copper plates with hand and power tools, he has interpreted Thornton's floral plates of twenty-four plants, also drawing on four other plates from different sources. Rather than colorful floral displays, Dine's flowers are painted in shades of black, white, and grey. Also emulating Thornton, each flower is juxtaposed with a tribute by a modern poet; on more obscure varieties, he has commissioned poems. Plath's poem, "Tulips," is used in this format. Plath is in a hospital following surgery for appendicitis; receiving a bouquet of red tulips, she expresses reluctance about being drawn back into the busyness of the everyday world when "I only wanted /To lie with my hands turned up and be utterly empty..." (UJ, 18).

63. Enid Mark (1932–2008). *About Sylvia*. Wallingford, PA: ELM Press, 1996. With lithographs by Enid Mark printed on Arches Velin paper, hand bound by Sarah Creighton in a chemise of black Tiziano paper from the Fabriano mill, and with title calligraphy by Jerry Kelly. One of 50 copies.

About Sylvia was conceived by Enid Mark, Sylvia Plath's classmate and friend, and founder of ELM Press. This artist's book was published during the tenth anniversary of the press, and contains ten poems by poets who either knew Plath personally or who reflect on her life and work from the distance of time. Its meaning for me is enhanced by having known and admired both of these women at a formative stage of our lives. Each of the poems, including those by Diane Ackerman, John Berryman, Robert Lowell, and Richard Wilbur, conveys personal recollections about Plath. The image of shattered glass shown here reflects the emotional depths of Robert Lowell's poetry; his Boston University workshop in 1959 introduced Plath to a boldly confessional mode of creative expression.

64. Georg Baselitz (b. 1938). *New Paintings. With Poems by Sylvia Plath and an Essay by Heinrich Heil.* London: Anthony D'Offay Gallery. Catalog raisonné to accompany an exhibition, 19 March–24 April 1999.

    Georg Baselitz (né Georg Kern) is an internationally recognized neo-expressionist painter, printmaker, and sculptor who was prominent in the revival of German expressionism and the incorporation of the human figure in painting. His paintings confront "the visceral reality of history and tragedy of being German in a post-World War II era."[61] Plath's well-documented preoccupation with her German ancestry as expressed in her poems about her father would have resonated with this artist. Seven of his inverted (upside-down) paintings dated 1998, emphasizing the ornamental background of a "sea of daisies upon which are drawn portions of reclining female nudes" alternate with seven of Plath's poems, in his words, "to paint pictures behind the canvas."[62] Shown is her poem, "The Moon and the Yew Tree."

65. Birtley Aris (b. 1927). Four-color serigraph illustrating the Sylvia Plath poem, "Among the Narcissi." Ashington, Northumberland (UK): Mid Northumberland Arts Group, June 1, 1971. MidNAG Poetry Poster No. 10.

Plath wrote this poem on April 5, 1962 about their friend and neighbor, Percy Key, who died of lung cancer that June. In the poem, she portrayed him with a walking stick, unsteady against the wind among their field of narcissi.

THEATRICAL PRODUCTIONS

66. Rose Leiman Goldemberg (b. 1929). *Letters Home: A Drama.* New York: Samuel French, 1980.

A play in two acts based on Aurelia Plath's edition of *Letters Home* (cat. 52). First produced by The American Place Theater in New York and also produced in England, Australia and other venues. This play is written from Aurelia's perspective, as she reads Sylvia's letters from college and from England, following her marriage to Ted Hughes. The play chronicles Aurelia's early life and turning points in her daughter's life: Sylvia's attempted suicide while in college, her graduation with honors, her Fulbright studies at Cambridge, marriage and separation from Hughes, and the birth of her children. The "dialogue" between mother and daughter evokes a fugue-like quality, ending with the telegram notifying Aurelia of Sylvia's death.

67. Barry Kyle (b. 1947). *Sylvia Plath: A Dramatic Portrait Conceived & Adapted from Her Writing.* London: Faber and Faber, 1976. Cover photograph by Donald Cooper.

The Royal Shakespeare Company production of *Sylvia Plath: A Dramatized Setting of Her Writings* (including her verse play *Three Women* presented in Act II) premiered in London for a seven-performance run from October 20–December 1, 1973. Directed by Barry Kyle, it featured a selection of Plath's poems and excerpts from her prose writings, presented in a biographical context. The RSC production moved to the Brooklyn Academy of Music in January 1974; Clive Barnes, the *New York Times* theater critic, wrote that "Miss Plath has taught me something about drama. Poetry is what drama is about. It is the hard core of the dramatic experience—everything else is peripheral...."[63] Faber and Faber published the play in book form three years after its London opening. It was not until January 2009, however, that another production of *Three Women* was staged in London, by the British director Robert Shaw, who moved it to New York City in October 2010 for a brief run.

68. Paul Alexander (b. 1955). *Edge*. Produced by Daryl Roth, performed at the DR2 Theatre, New York, August–September 2003. Theatre program.

A one-woman play starring Angelica Torn as Plath in what *The New York Times* called an "emotionally charged portrayal" of the poet as "a realist with an attitude" rather than a victim—one who is "tough, witty, and sarcastic, not the sort of woman who would take abuse lying down."[64]

69. The 19th New York International Fringe Festival presented two productions about Sylvia Plath from August–September 2016:

Plath. A New Musical. Presented by Fortress Productions, with performances on August 20, 23, 25, 27, 29, 2016 at the 14th Street Y in New York City. Music by Fernanda Douglas and book and lyrics by Molly Rose Heller. Theatre program.

This production had premiered as *Mad Girl's Love Song* at Columbia University at Barnard College in October 2014.

Nestor Caballero. *Musas.* A Water People Theater production performed in Greenwich Village, August 18–20, 2016. Theatre program.

In this two-character play, playwright Nestor Caballero imagines a conversation between Sylvia Plath and Frida Kahlo, their worlds colliding in a series of dream sequences.

70. *The Night Dances.* Dramatic readings of Plath poems, including the title poem, "The Night Dances," read by dramatic actress Charlotte Rampling; music by Benjamin Britten performed on cello by Sonia Wither-Atherton. Performed at the Park Avenue Armory, New York, April 22–26, 2015. Theatre program.

POETIC INTERPRETATIONS

71. Catherine Bowman. (b. 1957). *The Plath Cabinet.* New York: Four Way Books, 2009.

    In this collection of forty-four poems, Bowman celebrates Sylvia Plath's life and work based on both Plath's published and unpublished work and her research into the Plath materials held in the Lilly Library at Indiana University, Bloomington, where Bowman is the Ruth Lilly Professor of Poetry. This archive, which was acquired by the Lilly Library from Aurelia Plath, contains drafts, letters, photographs, and memorabilia from Sylvia's childhood that became a source of inspiration for Bowman, "an unofficial biography, an unofficial life."[65]

72. Sina Queyras. (b. 1963). *MxT.* Toronto: Coach House Press, 2014.

    Although the title of this collection presupposes a focus on scientific equations, Queyras uses it as a structure to write about the remembrance of things past. One section—"Emotion Frame Dimensions"—contains a series of elegies in the style of the eulogized subject, recalling images from a poet's work. Two elegies in this collection that incorporate images from Plath's poems are "Sylvia Plath's Elegy for Sylvia Plath" and "Elegy for Photographs Not Taken." In a forthcoming collection, *My Ariel* (Coach House Press, October

2017), Queyras reimagines Plath's iconic book, *Ariel* (cat. 8), exploring the cultural norms and archetypes that frame women's lives.

73. David Trinidad (ed.) (b. 1953). "Dossier: Sylvia Plath," in *Court Green 5*, Annual Issue. Chicago: Columbia College, 2008.

The title of this journal, *Court Green*, takes its name from the Devon home in which Plath and Hughes lived with their children. This issue features a dossier on the theme of Sylvia Plath. Contributions were sought that "pushed the boundaries of the epistle form, and poetry rooted in that tradition," as well as literary letters that were poetic.[66] Forty-nine poems, essays, and letters are included. Opened at Plath's poem, "Mirror," it is seen juxtaposed with Laura Mullen's response, "Mirror, Mirror" on the facing page. This journal, published from 2004 to 2015, will be delivered online as of fall 2017.

David Trinidad, co-founder of *Court Green*, is a contemporary poet and director of graduate programs in Fiction, Nonfiction and Poetry at Columbia College, Chicago. His anthology, *Dear Prudence: New and Selected Poems* (NY: Turtle Point Press, 2011), pays tribute to Plath in such poems as "Moon Street," "On Sylvia's Birthday," and "From Ted Hughes' List of Suggested Writing Exercises for Sylvia Plath."

74. Manfred Wolf (trans.) *On the Death of Sylvia Plath & Other Poems: Women's Voices from Holland & Flanders*. Berkeley: Two Windows Press, 1974. Signed by the printer; bound in ochre card cover.

The title poem is by Judith Frieda Herzberg, a Dutch poet who divides her time between the Netherlands and Israel. Herzberg was one of ten writers invited to contribute to Enid Mark's book, *About Sylvia* (cat. 63). She has also written two plays that have been made into films by Franz Weisz.

75. Howard Boatwright (1918–1999). *Five Poems of Sylvia Plath for Soprano and Piano.* Fayetteville, NY: Walnut Grove Press, 1995. Musical score.

   Five poems set to music: "New Year on Dartmoor," "Among the Narcissi," "Spinster," "Poppies in July," and "Poppies in October." Boatwright was an American composer, violinist, and musicologist and a pioneer in the performance of early choral music. He taught music composition and theory at Yale and Syracuse Universities.

76. Aribert Reimann. *Songs: Selections.* Munich: ORFEO International Music. Includes *Six Poems by Sylvia Plath* (1975) for soprano and klavier. CD, 2005.

   German composer, pianist and accompanist, known especially for his literary operas, including a German adaptation of Shakespeare's *King Lear.*

77. Ned Rorem (b. 1923) *Ariel: Five Poems of Sylvia Plath for Soprano, Clarinet and Piano.* New York: Boosey and Hawkes, 1974. Musical score.

   Composed in New York in May 1971 and presented by the composer as a gift to Phyllis Curtin, who performed the cycle with clarinetist David Glazer and pianist Ryan Edwards at the Library of Congress in Washington, DC on November 26, 1971. Recorded as "Ariel" (1971), which consisted of five poems by Sylvia Plath: "Words," "Poppies in July," "The Hanging Man", "Poppies in October," and "Lady Lazarus" (New York: Desto Records, 1973). Phyllis Curtin, soprano; Joseph Rabbal, clarinet; Ryan Edwards, piano.

78. Daryl Runswick. *Lady Lazarus for Amplified Female Voice; Text by Sylvia Plath.* London: Faber Music, 1991. Musical score.
   First performed by Judith Rees in Reykjavik on September 28, 1986.

NOTES

1] Sylvia Plath, "Ocean 1212-W," in Johnny *Panic and the Bible of Dreams, and Other Prose Writings.* (London: Faber and Faber, 1977), 130.

2] Helen Vendler. "Reconstructing the Colossus," Appendix: "Early Poems by Plath Treating Father's Death," in *Coming of Age as a Poet: Milton, Keats, Eliot, Plath.* (Cambridge, MA: Harvard University Press, 2004), 150–54.

3] Adrienne Rich. "Toward a Woman-Centered University," in *On Lies, Secrets, and Silence: Selected Prose, 1966–1978* (New York: Norton, 1976), 125–56.

4] Christopher Reid, ed., *Letters of Ted Hughes* (New York: Farrar, Straus and Giroux, 2007), 39.

5] Modern Language Association (MLA) database on *JStor* (accessed February 4, 2017).

6] Peter K. Steinberg, ed., *A Celebration, This Is* at www.sylviaplath.info and *Sylvia Plath Info Blog,* at http://sylviaplathinfo.blogspot.com.

7] Review of *Ariel,* by Sylvia Plath, "The Blood Jet is Poetry," *Time,* June 10, 1966: 118–20.

8] Webster Schott, review of *Winter Trees,* by Sylvia Plath, "The Cult of Plath," *Washington Post Book World,* October 1, 1972: 3.

9] Andrew Wilson, *Mad Girl's Love Song: Sylvia Plath and Life Before Ted* (New York: Scribner, 2013), 13-14.

10] Ibid., 80.

11] Hermione Lee, *Biography: A Very Short Introduction* (Oxford: Oxford University Press, 2009), 128–29.

12] Kathleen Spivack, "Poets and Friends," *Boston Globe Magazine,* August 9, 1981: 11.

13] Jane Baltzell Kopp, e-mail to Heather Clark, October 9, 2016. [Kopp's italics.]

14] Ibid.

15] Elizabeth Hardwick, "On Sylvia Plath," in *Ariel Ascending: Writings About Sylvia Plath,* ed. Paul Alexander (New York: Harper and Row, 1985), 105.

16] Vendler, *Coming of Age as a Poet,* 132.

17] A. Alvarez, review of *The Colossus*, by Sylvia Plath, "The Poet and the Poetess," *The Observer*, December 18, 1960: 22.

18] Sylvia Plath to Judith Jones, April 5, 1961, Harry Ransom Center, The University of Texas at Austin.

19] James Michie to Robert MacGregor, June 17, 1960 (see cat. 3).

20] Stephen Tabor, *Sylvia Plath: An Analytical Bibliography* (London: Mansell Publishing Ltd., 1987), vii.

21] Peter K. Steinberg, "Ingmar Bergman & Sylvia Plath," *Sylvia Plath Info Blog*, 1. http://sylviaplathinfo.blogspot.com/2007/07/ingmar-bergman-sylvia-plath.html (accessed 3/10/17).

22] Frieda Hughes, foreword to *Ariel: The Restored Edition*, by Sylvia Plath (London: Faber and Faber, 2004), x.

23] Robert Lowell, introduction to *Ariel*, by Sylvia Plath (New York: Harper and Row, 1966), ix.

24] "Script for the BBC Broadcast," in Appendix II to *Ariel, The Restored Edition*, by Sylvia Plath (London: Faber and Faber, 2004), 194.

25] Nancy D. Hargrove, "The Chronology of Sylvia Plath's Poems: 1956–1959," in *Studies in Bibliography*, vol. 45, 1992: 267, 275, 278, 285.

26] Wilson, *Mad Girl's Love Song*, 189.

27] Hargrove, *Chronology of Sylvia Plath's Poems*, 266.

28] Ted Hughes, *Birthday Letters* (London: Faber and Faber, 1998), 3.

29] Alex Kuczynski, "The Media Business: Goodbye to *Mademoiselle*: Condé Nast Closes Magazine," *The New York Times*, October 2, 2001: 1–3, http://www.nytimes.com/2001/10/02/business/the-media-business-goodbye-to-mademoiselle-conde-nast-closes-magazine.html (accessed May 12, 2013).

30] "Young Poets," *The Atlantic Monthly*, August 1955: 65.

31] Peter K. Steinberg, "Sylvia Plath's Circus Three Rings," *Sylvia Plath Info Blog*, http://sylviaplathinfo.blogspot.com/2017/3/sylvia-plaths-circus-three-rings.html (accessed March 23, 2017).

32] Editorial in *Gemini*, Spring 1957: 3.

33] Reid, *Letters of Ted Hughes*, 54.

34] Ted Hughes, "Notes on the Chronological Order of Sylvia Plath's Poems," *Tri-Quarterly* 7 (Fall 1966): 81–88.

35] Sylvia Plath, ed., "American Poetry Now," *Critical Quarterly Supplement* 2 (1961): 2.

36] A. Alvarez, "A Poet's Epitaph," *Observer Weekend Review*, February 17, 1963: 23.

37] Sylvia Plath, "Three Women: A Play for Three Voices," *Ms. The New Magazine for Women*, preview issue, January 1972: 88.

38] Tabor, *Sylvia Plath Bibliography*, 26.

39] Jonathan Bate, *Ted Hughes: An Unauthorized Life* (New York: Harper Collins, 2015), 105.

40] Hargrove, *Chronology of Sylvia Plath's Poems*, 268.

41] Reid, *Letters of Ted Hughes*, 39.

42] Ted Hughes, ed., introduction to *Johnny Panic and the Bible of Dreams* (New York: Harper & Row, 1979), 2.

43] Ibid, 7.

44] "Plath." *New York Times Book Review*, December 14, 1975: 37; reprinted in Tabor, 43.

45] Ibid.

46] Frances McCullough, "Advice and Consent," *Atlantic*, July 1976: 31.

47] D. H. Lawrence, *Complete Poems, Vol. II* (Surrey: Windmill Press, 1957), 204.

48] M. L. Rosenthal, "Poetry as Confession," *The Nation* 189 (1959), 154–55.

49] Robert Lowell, introduction to *Ariel*, by Sylvia Plath (New York: Harper & Row, 1966), xi.

50] Anne Sexton, "The barfly ought to sing," *Tri-Quarterly*, no. 7, Fall 1966: 92.

51] Sylvia Plath to Anne Sexton, February 5, 1961, Harry Ransom Center, The University of Texas at Austin.

52] Sylvia Plath to Anne Sexton, August 21, 1962, Harry Ransom Center, The University of Texas at Austin.

53] Heather Clark, e-mail to Judith Raymo, February 21, 2017.

54] Sylvia Plath, "Edith Sitwell," term paper, March 25, 1953, 27 (Plath mss. II, box 10, folder 7), Lilly Library, Indiana University.

55] Ibid, 1, 3, 5.

56] Sylvia Plath, "Alicante Lullaby," in *Collected Poems* (London: Faber and Faber, 1981), 47.

57] Ekbert Faas, *Ted Hughes: The Unaccommodated Universe* (Santa Barbara, CA: Black Sparrow Press, 1980), 210.

58] Leonard M. Scigaj, "'The Transparence of the Place in which He Is': The Influence of Stevens in Plath's Early Poems," 4 (research paper, Ted Hughes Papers, Series 3: Sylvia Plath, Subseries 3.5, Writings by Others, Stuart A. Rose Manuscript, Archives, and Rare Book Library, Emory University).

59] "Wallace Stevens, 1879–1955," *Poetry Foundation*: 5, http://www.poetry-foundation.org/poems-and-poets/poets/detail/wallace-stevens (accessed February 15, 2017).

60] Peter K. Steinberg, "Sylvia Plath's 'Mules That Angels Ride,'" *Sylvia Plath Info Blog*: 2, http//sylviaplathinfo.blogspot.com/2015/08/Sylvia-plaths-mules-that-angels-ride.html (accessed March 19, 2017).

61] "Georg Baselitz: Painter, Printmaker, Sculptor," *The Art Story*: 4, http://www.theartstory.org/artist-baselitz-georg.htm (accessed February 14, 2017).

62] Henrich Heil, introduction to *Georg Baselitz, New Paintings* (London: Anthony d'Offay Gallery), 7.

63] Clive Barnes, "Theater: 'Sylvia Plath,' Royal Shakespeareans Put Poet's Music and Insights Into Dramatic Setting," *The New York Times*, January 17, 1974: 44.

64] Anita Gates, "A Resurrected Sylvia Plath With No Saintliness, No Whining and Lots of Attitude," *The New York Times*, August 5, 2003: E5.

65] Catherine Bowman, *The Plath Cabinet*, New York: Four Way Books, 2009, 69.

66] David Trinidad, ed., "Call for Submissions," *Court Green* 5, 2008.

PRINTED IN THE CZECH REPUBLIC BY PB TISK. DESIGNED BY JERRY KELLY AND TYPESET IN HIS VOLTAIRE AND RILKE TYPEFACES.